Valhalla and the Fjörd:
A Spiritual Motorcycle Journey through the History of Strangford Lough

by
Peter Moore

GW00569102

Valhalla and the Fjörd:

A Spiritual Motorcycle Journey through the

History of Strangford Lough

Peter Moore

Clachan
Publishing

Clachan Publishing, Ballycastle, Glens of Antrim.

Valhalla and the Fjörd:

A Spiritual Motorcycle Journey through the History of Strangford Lough

Peter Moore

Clachan Publishing
3 Drumavoley Park, Ballycastle, BT54 6PE,
Glens of Antrim, Northern Ireland.

Email: info@clachanpublishing.com
Website: http://clachanpublishing-com.
ISBN — 978-1-909906-26-6

This edition published 2014,

www.moorso-begins.blogspot.co.uk
http://www.youtube.com/user/MoorsoP

Clachan
Publishing

About the Author

Peter studied archaeology and palæoecology in Queen's University, before specialising in maritime and marine archaeology in the University of Ulster. It was while there that he first engaged in archaeology inspired travel, with the university team traveling to Kenya, complete with film crew, to investigate the cultural maritime landscape at Mombasa.

It was whilst working in the Queen's University archaeological fieldwork unit that Peter honed his research of the archaeological record as well as report writing skills. Around this time, a lifelong friend and biker, who studied with Peter during his undergraduate degree, encouraged Peter to gain his motorbike license as well as giving him his first bike. The passion for archaeology and history was combined with motorbikes, it seemed a logical next step to write about this combination.

Peter lives with his fiancée, travels regularly to the Canary Islands to dive and make short underwater films on the wildlife there and records music with 'Portune Conspiracy'.

About Clachan Publishing

Clachan Publications is dedicated to preserving and promoting publications on Irish family and local history. We rely on local and family historians for much of our material and welcome submissions from them.

We also make available out-of-print and other rare books, enhancing them with notes, indexes and illustrations, where appropriate.

Acknowledgements

The cover image and all site and location photographs are by the author, unless otherwise stated.

Aerial Photography is by courtesy of Bing Maps, (www.bing.com) © Microsoft Corporation.

Thanks to Gavin Donaghy of Irish Archaeological Research Ltd for kind permission to use aerial images of Mahee Castle and the Mound of Down.

Abbreviations

ANT   a unique code given to County Antrim archaeological sites.

ASCD   Archaeological Survey of County Down

DOW   a unique code given to County Down archaeological sites.

MRD   a unique code given to every archaeological site by the Environment and Heritage Service. It tends to denote a site within the maritime landscape

NIEA   Northern Ireland Environmental Agency.

SMR   Site Monuments Record given by the Environment and Heritage Service's record of monuments in Northern Ireland.

Contents

Illustrations

Chapter One

Bikes and the Fjörd ∫ the long and winding road

Strangford Lough (Author)

Bikes and Strangford, what a combination! I had parked up at a small jetty to sit, have a cigarette and make some notes - as well as take in the beautiful scenery. I was wearing armoured leathers and the heat of that day in July was in sharp contrast to most days in this part of the world where angry blackened clouds can chase you down the road, adding a hurried dimension to the ride as well as a strange sense of foreboding. But today it meant that I was in danger of overheating; small beads of sweat were already uncomfortably running down my back. As I took my jacket off and opened a bottle of soft drink a voice came from behind.

"I went all round Ireland on a moped when I was sixteen." The face was world-weary, lined. He frowned as he examined the Triumph's engine, "I didn't have anything like that horsepower."

Thus spoke a stranger who felt compelled to come over and give me an account of his adventures. I couldn't help but listen. I wanted to ask questions and I could see in his eyes he clearly had stories to tell. This would be a good guy to go for a drink with, though it would be difficult to get a word in edgeways, yet the entertainment value would still be mighty. His solo travels as a young man were something I had never had the courage to undertake. It was only now, many years after my sixteenth birthday, that I was exploring my own country. He gazed wistfully over the water's surface. He loved Strangford, that much was clear. This, and his love of motorbikes, led me to ask myself whether he and I were similar spirits. I felt a sort of kinship with him, save the years between us.

"We live here now," he indicated by pointing at a phenomenal residence perched on the foreshore. Not bad for a sixteen-year-old Irish moped explorer! "And this is my wife."

No name was given so I politely shook hands and made my introduction. Still no name, so I could only smile awkwardly. She stood apart from her husband, the distance and almost tangible subservience noticeable, probably letting the 'men

2

talk' about engines and bikes, which obviously didn't interest her. She had come out for a walk around the lough, not to recount tales of youth, I could almost hear the sigh inside her head as she squinted to peer into the distance.

I had pulled over to get away from a caravaner who was hogging the narrow lanes, almost causing an accident at every turn. There were no caravan parks round this part of the lough, so why had they not unhitched the caravan before they drove here? Logic had, it seemed, escaped them. On more than one occasion I had muttered "selfish prick!" within my helmet - for all the good that would do. Irritation was then replaced with guilt at my lack of empathy!

I have come to biking relatively recently. At the time of writing I have been biking for about four or five years. Nonetheless, I have been on all sorts of terrain in Ireland and like to think I can handle a bike. I have never been into riding sports bikes - although I love watching Superbike racing, and the spectacular road racing we have here in Ireland. So, here I am writing about the sites and roads from the perspective of an 'adventure bike' rider. As I have not gone off-road, all you bikers out there, whatever you ride, can follow the routes I suggest and enjoy them. You will often see and hear, sports bikes on these roads. Ted Simon's books have been a huge influence on me, not just in terms of his writing but also his biking philosophy. He summed it up best when he said: *"Anything that travels very far very fast is scarcely worth transporting, especially the tourist"* (Simon, 1980). For me, the joy of a bike journey has never been about getting from A to B as fast as possible, although I do enjoy twisting the throttle from time to time.

The bike that I have used for my journeys around the lough and elsewhere is a Triumph Tiger 885i. The bike is the spoked wheel version with a nice smooth triple engine that has exceptional power delivery. Running Metzeler Tourance tyres the bike has a road bias, but I am capable of going up lanes and tracks without fear of a lack of grip or handling. I also like the bike's capabilities in the corners, there is plenty of 'poke' allowing for ease of overtaking.

As with most trips, it's always good to undertake them in good weather; it will add to the experience, although I have ridden these routes in all conditions, and it is always enjoyable. You can view videos of the roads to many of the sites on my YouTube channel.

A key aspect of biking for me is that some of the roads allow me time to contemplate and examine the darker side of my psyche as well the mistakes I have made, and the people I have hurt. Sometimes these self-examinations are painful, as reality sinks its teeth in. Frequently I say to myself *did I really say that?'* or *'why did I do that?'* More than once my eyes have closed for a nanosecond, I have let out a breath and moaned at the stupidity and selfishness of my actions. The ride is cathartic.

I have always found travelling down the lough shore, particularly the western shore, spiritually very moving, as well as mentally and emotionally relaxing. But the reason biking is so cathartic for me is I tend to use the time to self-examine. This tends to drive negativity and the dark thoughts from my head, but only when I have confronted them. On the bike around the lough I feel that I have stepped back in time somehow, although maybe leaving any urban sprawl for a more rural setting has this effect. But I become aware when I stop and sit in a quiet place that the trees and the foreshore have been here far longer than me, and will be around far longer after I am gone. It makes me realise how small I am, how insignificant in the greater scheme of things. The wind that invariably rustles the leaves is, for me, a comforting friend not quite telling me its secrets. The sound of gently lapping water somehow connects me to a primeval lineage; although, compared to the impact of modern man, the footsteps of our ancestors are like those of a ghost.

I think this is why I have chosen to write about my experiences, but more specifically about how the lough has

4

affected and helped me. Together with my motorbike, it has acted as a solace and helped me through difficult times. The historical sites around the lough's fringes are not only interesting in themselves, they are the places I usually find myself, either by accident or design, searching for the answers to my problems. Therefore for me, the lough, the motorbike and a sense of history go hand in hand.

I do not, for one minute, claim that this book is in any way a comprehensive guide to the history, archaeology or the best things to do around the lough; these are personal choices. I would however add a caveat - you *should* venture off the beaten track. For me, the excitement of any journey is discovering something - a place, a building or a view - that is off the 'tourist trail'. It is exploring for *myself* and I feel that even though the place has already been reported, recorded and photographed, I am somehow its discoverer. So, I encourage everyone to do the same.

Stop and chat to passersby, they tend to be a friendly bunch, and on a bike conversations with strangers seem to happen naturally anyway. I think the reason is that a bike is a symbol. A lot of people like the idea of the freedom a bike can give, they are perhaps even envious of the romanticism associated with it. The reality of being soaked to the bone never enters their heads, but the ethos does, and surely that is the most important thing. I also firmly believe that because bike riders are so exposed people, want to help us and are aware how vulnerable we can be. But there are occasions when even that vulnerability fades to nothing. When I sit at dawn or dusk on the shore overlooking some part of the water and the orange hued sun glints off it, I simply sit, breathe and reflect upon my life, while taking in the surroundings. At times the wind approaches from a distance, reaching a crescendo as it strikes the tree tops, like a crashing waves on a surf hit beach - enjoy and savor these moments!

The terrain becomes more spread out as one leaves the more urbanised areas. The villages around the lough remain quaint, and most of the pubs agreeably traditional. Some of the roads are occasionally made more challenging by tractors dragging mud onto the tarmac surface, but these form part of the charm and uniqueness of the area.

For those who have never visited the area, I can say that Strangford Lough is, arguably, one of the most beautiful natural landscapes in Western Europe and, on a good day, perhaps, in the world; and one that has had for millennia engaged and fascinated mankind. It remains an area of scientific and biological importance and is currently a Marine Natural Reserve, but is significant culturally, historically and archaeologically as well. For these reasons there is a considerable lobby to have it designated a World Heritage Site.

The lough has been used by mankind for millennia. The most obvious evidence of this is its very name. Strangford Lough is a derivative of the Norse Strangr-fjǫrðr or Strandfjörthr meaning 'The Strong Fjörd', referring to the exceptional tidal forces located at the lough narrows. The Viking and Early Christian eras both in timeline and common myth are seen as going hand in hand here, and I suppose in a way they do, but the Vikings are something of an obsession of mine as they genuinely fascinate me. Valhalla (from Old Norse Valhöll meaning 'hall of the slain') is an enormous hall located in Asgard (one of the Nine Worlds and home to the Æsir tribe of gods), and is ruled over by the Viking god Odin. Chosen by Odin, half of the Viking warriors who die in combat travel to Valhalla upon death, led by valkyries, while the other half go to the goddess Freyja's field Fólkvangr. Valhalla is, in essence, the Viking heaven. It seems appropriate then that the title of this book not only references the Norse origin of the name Strangford, but as travelling the lough represents a heaven of sorts for me, using Valhalla as part of the title seemed appropriate.

The earliest Celtic or Irish name for the area is Louch Cuan meaning 'Lough of the Harbours', which refers to the shallows, mud flats and abundance of landing places (Forsythe et al, 2002, 2).

6

The Triumph parked on the jetty (Author)

The tidal forces the Norse name refers to *are* exceptional - believe me, as I have felt their full force whilst scuba diving in the lough. At times I was hanging on to anything in sight in a freakish almost cartoony way, sucking the air out of my scuba tank at an alarming rate. After all, 350 million cubic metres of water enter and exit the lough through the Narrows with the passing tides.

To return to the history of the lough, the earliest human activity around the foreshore dates to the Mesolithic (approximately 7000 BC – 9000 years ago) with shell middens – basically rubbish mounds – found at several locations including Millen Bay and Rough Island.

The site at Rough Island, excavated in the early 20th Century, also uncovered an abundance of flint finds, including microliths, Bann flakes and scrapers. In essence these are different classifications of flint objects classed by their shape or function. Bann flakes, for instance, are usually leaf-shaped flint blades dating from the Late Mesolithic period (6000-4500 BC). They are named after the Bann River in Northern Ireland and part of the Bann culture assemblage. If you stop to think about that for a moment this in itself is an astounding fact; long before the Egyptian Pyramids, our ancestors were living round the shores of the lough. It's not surprising though, as the lough would have offered an abundance of natural resources as well as food, with the marine life providing much needed protein, and the foreshore and land immediately behind probably providing ample foraging habitats.

The Viking and Early Christian eras both in timeline and common myth are seen as going hand in hand here, and I suppose in a way they do. However, I intend to discuss the history of each location in more detail in the relevant chapters. But chronologically you can easily find sites and remains from all eras of human history, and all relatively close to each other – either by accident or design.

Chapter Two

Journeys Begin ∫ Comber to Sketrick

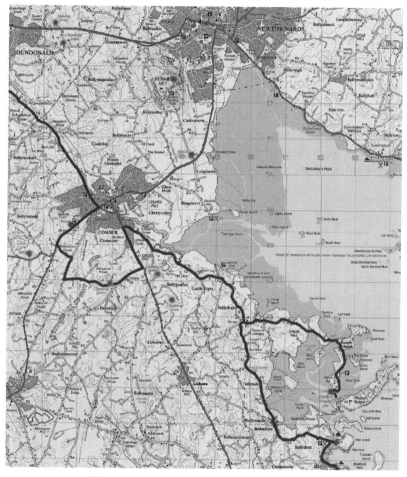

Suggested Route from Comber to Sketrick Castle

I have already made an assumption that anyone wishing to follow this rough guide will be arriving at the area from a Belfast direction. If you are not, then I ask your indulgence, this is the route by which I always approach the area so it seemed logical to me!

The first town encountered is Comber. Although its centre has seen some regeneration in recent years, the town appears to me to have a slightly 'tired' appearance. It was once an industrial hub containing flour, saw and bleach mills, as well as several distilleries. One of the old mills has, as is so often with old mills and warehouses these days, been turned into what appears to be rather swanky apartments. The name Comber is derived from the Irish *An Comar* meaning 'a confluence' (NIPNP, 2008, 24). The confluence refers to the meeting or junction of two rivers and this sort of place name is common throughout Ireland (O'Laverty, 1847, 197).

There are records of a Cistercian monastic site in the town on the site of the current St. Mary's parish, situated at an angle between the Enler and Glen rivers, referred to as both *Comerarium* and *Comor* (ASCD, 1966, 289). The Comber Historical Society suggests that when built, the monastic site would have been on virgin ground and was a standalone site. Records indicate the monastery was built in 1199, under the patronage of *Brian Catha Dun* or *Catha an Dúna*, meaning [of the] Battle of Down – referring to a battle that occurred in Downpatrick.

> ...in 1201, the founder had the misfortune to cross swords with de Courcy and perish in the conflict. The Abbey was occupied by monks from Caermarthernshire and it flourished until such establishments were dissolved by Henry VIII. In 1543, the last Abbot, John O'Mullegan resigned the Abbey and its possession to the Crown. It has seven townlands – Ballymonster, Carnesure, Cullintraw, Cattogs, Troopersfield, Ballynichol and half of Ballygowan. (Nevin, 2009, 1).

There appears to be some dispute about dates, as the Battle of Downpatrick between Brian O'Neill (*Brian Ua Néill*) is

10

recorded as taking place in 1260 not 1201, but the early foundations are probably 12th Century.

There are some quaint coffee shops situated off The Square in Comber, and even though my Grandparents are buried in Comber cemetery, it is not a place I have ever had a tendency to linger in. My adult memories of the place are of standing forlorn in front of black marble with inset gold lettering, while remembering pottering about with my Grandfather in his tool shed and later wishing I had known him in my adulthood.

The archaeology of the surrounding area is also interesting. I carried out an excavation at Islandhill, just outside Comber close to the cemetery on the shores of the lough near Rough Island. Although mainly a monitoring exercise for the building of a car park, there was a prehistoric axe head recovered as well as post holes. But its proximity to Rough Island is perhaps more significant, suggesting an active prehistoric landscape in this area. Now there isn't much to see, although at low tide you can walk across to Rough Island.

The first site I encountered is the motte on the outskirts of Comber to the south west (refer to the map on the chapter cover page). If travelling from Belfast turn right onto the A21 (Ballygowan Road) before entering Comber town proper. In a field approximately one kilometre on the right hand side is a tight circle of trees (usually an indication of something!). The motte is visible from the roadside and there is a track up to the site, but access is via the adjacent farm. As a matter of courtesy I knocked on the door and asked permission to use the track as the site is on the farmer's land. I advise you do the same. I am always amazed at how far basic manners can get you!

A motte is a raised earth mound fortification on which would normally have stood a palisade and tower. The fortification was a favourite of conquering Anglo-Normans as they spread their territories, being relatively quick to erect. The design was first used when the Normans conquered England and Wales after 1066. It is widely accepted they came to Ireland in the

12th and 13th Centuries. Sometimes the mounds were accompanied by a lower enclosure called a bailey which would have been an enclosed courtyard. There are some exceptional and impressive examples and there are also smaller mounds that can be slightly underwhelming. This site, alas, falls into the latter category, and it makes me wonder if it is, in fact, a raised rath rather than an Anglo-Norman fortification. An old mentor of mine, Dr Tom McNeill, seems to have it marked on his map as a possible motte but it remains questionable (McNeill, 1975, 50). Although the exact classifications still draws debate, ring-forts, raised raths and small mottes can be confused and, even when inspected on the ground, can appear very similar. This may seem a little over the top for anyone not engaged in an academic study of them and the simple question remains, once off your bike and standing on top of them, do you really care? I don't! All that matters is that the trees provide shade and/or shelter and there is somewhere to sit!

From the top, I noticed that the site is now much truncated; time and modern man have wizened and shrunken the mound, unsympathetic to the thousand years or so that it had stood proud. To the west of the site are lovely views over open countryside, but from this site, I had a sense of a limited horizon and found myself restless to get back on the bike.

I continued on the A21 heading roughly south before taking a left turn for the Old Ballygowan Road which runs parallel to the more modern road. It is agreeably more quiet and narrow than the main A21. The field hedgerows rise higher than any vehicle seating position and give me the sensation of travelling in a tunnel, but not in a claustrophobic way. Their proximity also gives a greater sense of speed, even when not travelling very fast. The road is smooth but undulating and the crests and dips add to the fun. Although I film many of the bike rides with a Go Pro set up, I don't tend to stop to take pictures of the road, so the photos which appear here are taken from Google's 'Street View' (Tele Atlas, 2009).

View of the Old Ballygowan Road (Tele Atlas, 2009, © Google Maps)

Approximately two kilometres on is a right turning for the Ballynicol Road. Roughly one and a half kilometres on from this turning is a curiosity. At first, you could be forgiven for missing it or mistaking it for a garden ornament or folly, but it makes an ideal quick stop (especially if the bike suspension is a bit soft). In someone's front garden are the remains of a prehistoric court tomb, now a group of five standing stones in a rough arc known locally as the 'Five Sisters' or 'The Hand of Jacks'. Again, if you want to get up close, as these are on someone's private land, I'd advise knocking their door and asking permission. But they are so close to the road it isn't really necessary to go into the garden to get a good look at them.

The facade of a court tomb is all that remains of the Neolithic monument. Excavation in 1955 showed that the burial gallery had been deliberately destroyed sometime in the not-recent past by the stones having been buried in a ditch that had been dug along the axis of the gallery. (Dunlop, 2009, 12).

The road forks, but keep left onto the Drumhirk Road, taking the A22 Killinchy Road north back towards Comber. A sign for Nendrum and a turn off to the right onto the Ballydrain Road should be clearly visible. This, in my opinion, is where the lough trip *really* starts. The road instantly narrows, the surface is rougher in texture but no less forgiving, this gives enough grip, allowing a quick pace on a bike.

Though so close to Comber, this road always immediately transports me into the countryside, my senses (especially if it's a hot day) are assaulted. I don't know if the position of the sea lough has an effect, but it smells like the south of France, or certainly how I remember the south of France to smell, with the heat increasing the fragrance of wildflowers, the sweet scent pervading my nostrils. I know it sounds peculiar, but I think there is also a smell from the warm tarmac which is somehow reassuring. The way the tyres bite to give excellent grip gives me increased confidence on the twisty corners. The road undulates and turns, barricaded by field hedgerows and I can't help but smile beneath my helmet.

When there is positive camber a bike can really be 'thrown' around, as it tacitly accepts the loads placed on the suspension. The sporadic outcrops of gorse smell of coconut and the reflection of their bright yellow flowers can be a distraction. However, a word of warning; beware of tractors pulling out of fields and also the occasional good citizen cutting the grass fringes close to their properties. The reason I like these roads in summer is that, later, - when the weather becomes wetter - these tractors pull a lot of mud onto the roads, which is something to bear in mind.

The views are only rarely visible through field gates or breaks in the hedgerows, but the lure of the glimpses of a blue mass of water as it shimmers in sunlight is like a primeval calling. I find the throttle twisting ever further towards me on the straights, my head tilts down and my stare fixes ever harder with concentration. At these times my mind is blank; no other thoughts enter except the road, the upcoming bend, the smells and the feel of the machinery working underneath me. *Enjoy this, as a Zen-like state has been achieved*!

If you travel on this road, you will arrive at a road fork and junctions, again following the signs for Nendrum, turn left, but remember this route, as you will double back to this junction and take the other road in due course. You will now be on the Ringneill Road, heading roughly east. At certain places, the lough shoreline laps up close to the road side; the views open up as a result. Just before the causeway is a jetty, protruding agreeably into the blueness of the lough. This is where I have pulled over many times and I suggest you do the same. Dangle your feet over the edge and relax, maybe letting your engine tick cool. The causeway is even narrower, with a low stone wall on either side. Once you are off this, the road bends to the right at almost ninety degrees – be careful not to go straight on (as I have done) - this is someone's driveway! The end of the causeway marks the beginning of Reagh Island with the road hugging the east shoreline which leads to the next destination: Mahee Island.

There are a few tempting laneways, but these are onto private land; as at Cross Island. Don't take them! Over a blind crest is another much smaller causeway that leads to Mahee Island; Mahee is the largest island within the lough and it is thought the name is derived from *Mochaoi,* a saint associated with Nendrum Monastic Site (Macdonald, 2002, 1). The island's archaeological history is a microcosm for the lough, with finds from the Mesolithic through to the 19th Century building of the causeway and everything in between.

Once over the crest you are greeted immediately by the sight of Mahee Castle (sometimes referred to as Nendrum Castle) which is a little over-restored for my tastes. However, I had the good fortune to be part of, if only briefly, an excavation here in 2002.

Aerial view of Ringneill Road to Reagh Island and Mahee Island (Bing Maps) ©
Microsoft Corporation

The castle has traditionally been dated to 1570 under the patronage of Captain Thomas Browne, although the report from the 2002 excavations, of which I was a part, recommends caution regarding this traditional belief, arguing that:

> Too much weight has been placed upon the historical evidence for dating Mahee Castle contained in Brown's petition. It is not even certain that the petition refers to Mahee Island. Provisional analysis of the dating evidence recovered during the 2002 excavations suggests a date range somewhere within the fifteenth to sixteenth centuries for the construction and occupation of the tower house. Although this evidence is consistent with the c.1570 date conventionally derived from Brown's petition, there is no reason that the construction of the tower house could not be significantly earlier within this period. (Macdonald, 2002, 31).

Aerial Image of Mahee Castle (Image taken by and used with kind permission of Gavin Donaghy of Irish Archaeological Research Ltd.)

The argument is that the tower house could have been built earlier, but it probably dates to sometime in the 16th Century.

There is nowhere to stop safely at the castle, but a car park for Nendrum is only 100 metres to the south, so I would advise parking there and walking to the castle to have a look around. I like to do this on my own, as I have never been a fan of exploring places surrounded by other people. Mahee Castle, though, isn't really explored an awful lot, certainly when I have been there, so this shouldn't be a problem. I like sitting towards the northern end of the castle with the causeway on my right looking out over the lough. A stillness pervades my mind when I do this – I usually light a cigarette to help with the ambiance.

There are many who would say that the jewel in the crown of the area is Nendum Monastic Site. Who am I to argue? The site is one of the best examples of an Early Christian monastic site in Ireland. There is ample parking at the bottom of the site fronting the lough and the view, even from here, is simply breathtaking, and I have used it for the cover image of this book. The main site sits atop the hill. Medieval records say it was founded in the 5th century as the date for the death of the

17

Saint, *Mochaoi,* is recorded between 490 and 497 (Reeves, 1847, 148), but this is uncertain and there is some debate as to whether Nendrum was a full monastery in the 5th century or whether it developed in the 6th century; one suggestion is that *Mochaoi* was a missionary bishop who initially had his base here (NIEA, 2005, 1).

There are frequent references to Nendrum in the Annals of Ulster, the earliest I could find was from 639AD referencing the

> ...repose of *Crídán* in *Naendrium* and of *Aed Dub,* abbot of Cell Darra – both bishops. (Bambury *et al,* 2000 U639.4.2).

Interestingly, there is also a reference to a death which some argue was a result of an attack by the Vikings in 976 AD, in which,

> *Sétna ua Demáin,* superior of *Naendruim,* was burned to death in his own house. *(Ibid,* 976.5).

The monastic site at Nendrum was discovered by Reeves in 1844 whilst he was conducting research. Since Reeves' initial work at the site there have been four phases of excavation at Nendrum. The one of perhaps most significance was conducted by H.C. Lawlor who oversaw an excavation. But more importantly, he also conducted a programme of restoration work at the site between 1922 and 1924 on behalf of the Belfast Natural History and Philosophical Society. The rebuilt and restored round tower and other monuments are what are visible today.

The site is defined by three large concentric cashels (circular dry stone walls) largely rebuilt by Lawlor. In the south-west segment of this enclosure is a series of circular and oval platforms. Excavated finds suggest that these were work-shops, including a bronze-smith's hut. The inner cashel on top of the hill contains the remains of a rectangular gabled church, a round tower and a graveyard, while the second cashel contains the so-called monastic school or workshop and further burials (Macdonald, 2003, 3). The plan of Nendrum published in Macdonald's report shows how comprehensive the site is.

Between 1995 and 2000 a series of excavations were undertaken within the lough and immediate foreshore near the car park for the site. What was uncovered was astounding; three phases of tidal mill associated with the monastic site were excavated; the earliest of which dated to 619 – 621AD making them the earliest tidal mills in Europe or Asia (McErlean et al, 2007, 63).[1] There isn't much to see on the ground so your imagination will have to suffice, but the site is so much more than a church and tower on top of a hill.

When I have visited, it has tended to be early or late summer and the slopes leading up to the site have been covered in bluebells. I usually stop at the car park area, not yet entering the place, and sit for a moment in quiet contemplation. The sun splits the trees and that familiar rustle of the foliage returns to comfort me. For one brief moment it feels as though my life has led me to this place. The sense of spirituality - note, I said spirituality, not religion or Christianity - is palpable, and at times heavy in the air and on my senses. I look up to the round tower stump as I carefully trudge my way to the top in motorbike boots. As I walk further towards the top, the breeze off the lough becomes fresher, occasionally whistling off the remains, adding to the atmosphere an almost eerie quality. There can be families and tourists on the site; I prefer to take myself away from them, amazing how their presence feels like some sort of intrusion.

I enjoy being able to run my hands over the remains; I am literally touching history. I can feel the carved stone of the sundial knowing that it was an important functional object over a thousand years old. The views from the site are panoramic, Portaferry lies to the south east and I enjoy observing the ferry chugging its way over to Strangford town, waging its battle against the currents with every last nut and bolt straining at

---

[1] The tidal mill excavation uncovered, amongst other finds, a millstone. Tide mills

the inevitable victory. I stare into the distance and an infinity of nothingness enters and clears my mind - my eyes slowly close – peace at last! The site seems to exude some force, as if there is a multitude of souls in the very stones that comprise the buildings. I don't know if this is the philosophy of Pandeism or Pantheism, but in the tranquility of the moment, I don't care.

The sun splitting the trees at Nendrum (Author)

It is possible, I suppose, to cover the entire lough in a day; but that would be something of a whistle stop tour, so I strongly advise taking time over it and, if you are lucky enough to live locally, splitting it into several days. If you are not a Strangford-ian then there are plenty of camp sites, B&B's and small hotels that can cater for your needs. I have been on bike trips with friends in other locations where we wild-camped (always the way to do it I think!) but the laws are slightly different here, so seek permission as you could land yourself in a bit of hot water!

20

The church ruins and sundial at Nendrum (Author)

The reconstructed Round Tower and dry stone wall at Nendrum (Author)

21

On leaving Nendrum. I feel like I'm being wrenched away; away from the views and the aura. If you are following this route there is no choice but to take the road you came on, back to the causeway off Reagh Island to the Ringneill Road. At the junction I described earlier, bear left briefly onto the Quarry Road, then take an immediate left onto the Tullynakill Road, following the signs for Ardmillan. The turnoff is marked by an old schoolhouse on the corner, now with a plaque above the door notifying that it is the 'Ballydrain Harrier and Athletic Club'. The Tallynakill Road is in the finest tradition of the Irish 'B' or country road – the surface is good (in the main) and the bends agreeably long and sweeping. However, the second time I rode here I realised how technically challenging the road can be. With many corners and blind bends, coupled with rising crests, it can make for some trail braking moments. On these occasions I corner adjusting the power, feathering the throttle and gently applying the rear brake. There are long straights where I take advantage of some of a bike's ample horsepower, although given that most of the road is partially enclosed by field hedgerows, seeing what's round the corners can prove difficult. On more than one occasion a bend has been more severe than I had anticipated and the road has outfoxed me; just as well the oncoming lane was clear!

Behind the hedgerows are open fields and this somehow translates to an open and 'airy' feeling on the bike - a release that is utter freedom! Occasionally small birds dart out from the hedges, which can give a heart-in-the-mouth moment, I am sure some of them sometimes misjudge the distance and pace. I have looked up at times and seen a bird of prey, usually a buzzard, riding a thermal, gliding in magnificence above my head. There is one that circles above my house especially in the autumn with its distinctive cry that pierces the air. I wonder is it my spirit guide somehow watching over and guiding me.

Through a break in the trees, on the left hand side, grey stone stands out strikingly against the shades of green. The roofless structure, providing an intriguing silhouette against the sky as it peeps over the low trees, is Tullynakill Church. There is a small 'D' shaped area to the side of the road where one can park which also acts as the site marker. On the occasions I have visited the site I have always been alone - the only visitor to a site that isn't signposted or well known. The whole site has a cramped feel to it. I get the distinct feeling there are ghosts among the buried there; some no doubt have scores that need settled or misdeeds clarified. As I stroll I read headstone inscriptions from families who have lost so many young children; one family losing four children all at the age of four. How horrific would that be?

The name Tullynakill is an Anglisation of *Tulaigh na Cille* meaning 'knoll of the church'. Genealogists are fascinated by the early headstone inscriptions in the adjoining graveyard, with many trying to trace ancestry by using them as a starting point. It is nice to wander the graveyard and read the inscriptions from the 17th and 18th centuries. They tell tales of lives lived as well as tragedies encountered. I have never found graveyards scary or unsettling places, maybe because during my higher education courses we were forever walking round them. But I think the aspect I like is the human stories that they add to any stop - they somehow make the past more easily accessible, tangible and more real.

The history and development of the site is interesting and it appears to have superceded Nendrum. The papal taxation of 1306 lists Nendrum as a parish church and, at some point in the Middle Ages, parish worship was moved to Tullynakill and the island site of Nendrum was abandoned (NIEA, 2005, 2). The Discover Northern Ireland tourist website states:

> Tullynakill was built in the late Middle Ages ... It is around 1450 when the last references to a church at Nendrum can be found. (http://www.discovernorthernireland.com).

The site at Nendrum does, certainly, appear to have fallen into disuse and possibly even ruin by the 15th century, so there may well have been some site or transitional site at Tullynakill then or slightly later, but the current structure and historical records appear to date it to later.

> Reeves noted in the mid-19th century the ruins of a 17th-century church next to the one then in use in Tullynakill townland (ruin dated 1639 of church 'on a little hill, opposite to the island', EA 197). The descriptive name Tullynakill makes its appearance in the 1615 Terrier of church property as well as on the secular Raven maps of c.1625. (Muhr, 2008, NIPNP).

The Sites and Monuments Record (SMR) states that the site became the parish for Nendrum in the 15th century, suggesting that there was some sort of site in the 15th or 16th centuries with renovation in the 17th century (SMR, 1992, DOW017:003).

Other sources also state that the current ruins probably date to the 1600's, but are situated on the site of a much older church. Writing in 1856, Getty refers to the 1291 Taxation of Pope Nicholas IV which:

> Enumerates all the parishes and chapelries in Ireland, arranged under their several dioceses and rural deaneries. Accordingly, among the churches in the diocese of Down, and in the rural deanery of Blaethwye, the 'Ecclesia de Nedrum' is introduced between Kilwyinchi [Killinchy,] and Kilmode [Kilmood,] a position corresponding to that which the modern parish of Tullynakill occupies on the county map. (Getty, 1856, 137).

This further suggests that there may have been a religious site here in the medieval period; in any case the current remains provide an intriguing and peaceful place to visit.

Although not apparent from the church site, an island situated in the lough to the east of Tullynakill called Wood Island has a structure on it visible in the aerial photographs and it is marked on the Ordnance Survey First Edition maps (1829 – 1835). I have tried to carry out research into what this is as I had thought it possibly the remnants of another island church site, akin to the likes of Chapel Island. I would stress it is hard to tell specifics from the aerial image and it could simply be a cottage or buildings associated with agricultural activity; but

24

that it has remained *in situ* that long did rouse my curiosity. I discovered that a census from 1841 records a population of four on the island. With this information I could be swayed from the idea of it being a religious site type. However, the Sites and Monuments Record record it as a 'sub-rectangular structure' (MRD168:019) but that's about it – the mooted date is 'uncertain' - mysterious indeed! Further research also records a prehistoric shell midden on the island (MRD168:179). The Second Edition maps highlight a fording causeway accessible at low tide, but I have never attempted to cross to the island and I am unsure about its ownership, so would advise the same caution. I often wish I had access to a small boat. I think sailing the lough and stopping at small outcrops and islands would be a great adventure, and heaven only knows what one would stumble across - maybe that could be a second book!

Tullynakill Church (Author)

Architectural detailing at Tullynakill Church (Author)

Headstone dating to 1760 at Tullynakill Church (Author)

If you continue south on the Tullynakill Road, remember to enjoy the tight lines that it requires, for just over a kilometre before filtering left onto the slightly larger (I use the term very loosely) Ardmillan Road. Before this is a small hamlet called Ardmillan with a drumlin hill directly in front of the road rising up into the sky. When planted with crops they sway gracefully in the breeze.

As the road passes the more modern houses the hamlet deteriorates aesthetically, but a remnant from the past – a bright red telephone box – still stands proud. A lot of the houses are modern and they exhibit, to me, no sense of place or context in the landscape. The whole hamlet seems to be alien amongst the rolling drumlins, an interruption to the flow of the land and represents a stark illustration of our impact on the natural world. I find on any bike journey a more heightened sense of 'oneness' with what is around me, the irony isn't lost on me; I know I am on a man-made machine that is emitting pollutants, but it doesn't make this sensation any less real. Maybe it is because of this awareness that I have become more conscious of the ugliness that mankind creates and the selfishness of our species, as well as our apparent inability to live in harmony with the ebb and flow of nature.

Once through the hamlet, there is a beautiful river that flanks the left side of the road with trees lining its path. At this point the road visually appears to narrow, however, breaks in the trees reveal fields on the right and open the sky up again. The river looks like it might have trout but, as I am no angler, I could be horrifically mistaken! At the next junction, the choice of which way to turn is entirely up to you as a traveller on your own journey; you can veer right on the Ballydorn Road, following the signs for Ballydorn and Whiterock, or continue straight on the Killinakin Road. The latter is more of a 'green lane' or tarmac track and if you enjoy the adventure style bikes this is the one to take. If you are on a more road orientated bike I would suggest the Ballydorn Road, which is also perhaps more scenic.

The Killinakin Road rises and falls with the bike suspension almost bottoming out before lifting over the crests. For me this is an exceptionally joyful experience, my heart rate seems to increase with the excitement and a stupid dumb grin becomes etched on my face. In places the trees arch over the road, providing a green tunnel that also serves to focus my attention ever harder on the road. The air rushes in through the vents in my helmet or through an open visor and I find that I have become part of the machine. The corners seem to flow, and the bike becomes an extension of my body. I lean in and the machine complies with the direction of my eyes, which are firmly fixed on the next apex. I can't say I've ever scraped the footpegs on these roads but I have had the bike cranked over, thankfully the Tourances providing excellent grip.

One of the advantages of these routes is that they can be taken at a sedate pace or they can be travelled quite quickly. However, I have been influenced by bike adventurers like Ted Simon and Sam Manicom. Their philosophy is to view the interruptions as the journey more than the road time itself. I think if you view any trip this way it is much more rewarding and potentially fulfilling. When I have taken a pillion, this more sedate approach has been taken as a lack of experience has required it. Frequent stops are not something to view negatively.

If you turn left at the end of this road along the Whiterock Road, the better surface and wider expanse means a more relaxing ride that requires slightly less concentration. I tend to take in the views, as once the top of the drumlin is reached, there is a descent to the bay and the lough laps up against the stone revetment wall. At this point there is a causeway to the next stop - Sketrick Castle.

Sketrick Castle is a towerhouse type monument approached by a causeway onto Sketrick Island, surrounded by the familiar green of the Environment and Heritage Service's fences and signs. The castle is thought to date to the 15th century; it stood fairly complete until 1896 when a storm damaged the structure. It was previously a four storey high building with a boat bay, lock up and subterranean passage. The Irish Annals record the castle being taken in 1470. The Annals of the Four Masters record:

> O'Neill on this occasions made a prisoner of Art, the son of Donnel Cael O'Neill and took the castle of Sgath-deirge which he delivered up into the keeping of Mac Quillan. (Hondelink, 2002, 1067).

The Annals of Ulster record:

> Art, son of Domnall Ua Neill the Slender, was slain there and the castle of Sgathdergi was obtained on that expedition by Ua Neill and he gave it into possession of Mac Uibhilin to keep it. And Ua Neill went to his house from that expedition with triumph of victory and rout. (Balé et al, 2003, U1470.2).

To be honest there isn't all that much to see. If there were once any other associated structures or earthworks they have long since gone with development allowed to take place alarmingly close to the castle.

The iron steed parked in front of the ruins of Sketrick Castle (Author)

The restaurant 'Daft Eddies' is located directly beside the castle and the site as a whole is popular with tourists, picnickers and dog walkers, so there is no pervading sense of calm or stillness, rather a perturbing bustle. The castle feels like it has been air lifted into a more modern scene rather than creating the impression that everything else there has grown up around it. I guess that this is, generally, part of a more developed area of the lough, close to other towns. But the juxtaposition between it and other sites is stark. As a result, it is hard to contextualize the site and I can't imagine the significant battles that it was associated with and there is no sense of 'place' associated with its position. Anytime I have been I have taken myself off for a walk round the quays and the lough shore. Once several dogs that were not mine decided to tag along, which made for some entertainment, then again, a Spaniel always seems to be quite entertaining with its ears flopping back as it darts about. But I felt an urgency to get back on the bike and leave; the number of people around made me feel uncomfortable. But that is my problem and my perception, rather than any fault of theirs.

Chapter Three

West side ∫ Killinchy to Walshestown

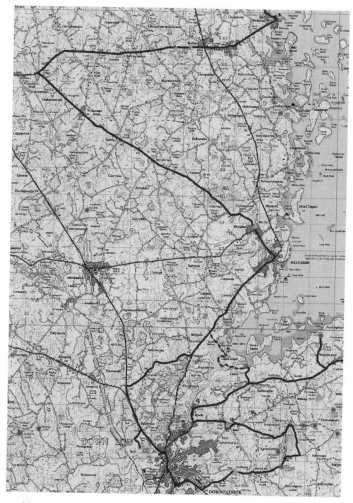

Map showing the suggested route from Whiterock to Walshestown

On leaving Sketrick, the road to take is the arrow straight A22 Comber Road via Killinchy. The village of Killinchy comes from the Irish *Cill Duinsí or* 'Duinseach's church'. The village probably grew up around the church, which is listed in the 1306 Papal Taxation as *Ecclesia de Kilwyinchi*, a name which Reeves explained as *Cill Insi* or church of the island. I came across an excavation report which records that in 1842 there was a coin hoard of 500 pennies of Henry III unearthed here, (Carruthers, 1853, 165). Like so many places though, not just in this locality, what where once small hamlets or market towns and villages now seem lost within the modern landscape – at least that is my impression. Poor architectural choices, especially in the 1960's, and the realization of the importance of our cultural heritage occurring too late in the consciousness of the statutory agencies and, I suppose, society as a whole, has meant that the character and context of these small villages has gone. All too often there is a road running through the middle of them and they are simply something that flies by in our peripheral vision; these small villages in themselves not usually being the destination. Hindsight is a wonderful thing – God only knows I am aware of that! – and I know it seems easy for me to criticise decisions that people thought were best at the time. But it doesn't make that criticism any less valid.

Once through Killinchy and onto the Comber Road, the next landmark is another small hamlet called Balloo. Again, this consists pretty much of one main street, but it offers an opportunity to stop for coffee or tea at Balloo House. Next you may head straight for the Saintfield Road, following the signs for Saintfield. This is a road I came across quite by accident and, to my mind, is a lovely, albeit quite short, road for a motorbike. I have only taken it in the summer and my memory of it is rose-tinted; with the smells of tree blossom in the air, as well as something I can't quite describe, but liken to warm grass – probably from the fields adjoining the road. It has always been agreeably empty and I have to be honest and say I have tended to fly along it, although at one point on the crest of a hill is a blind left hand corner with slight negative camber. The first time I was on the road this nearly caught me out; the forks divided as I had to make what I suppose would be classed as an emergency stop of sorts. There are sites of possible interest lining the road, mostly raths, but not easily accessible and, in truth, there is not always a lot to see, so for this road, I advise simply enjoying the ride.

The road has great undulations and there is a section that plunges through a wood, the tarmac splitting the trees like a sharp axe. When shrubs encroach on the road they sometimes flick off my arm, leaving sticky pollen residue on my leathers – a 'battle' scar! As I twist the throttle back, my grin gets wider as my weight leans and shifts the bike with ease.

At the end of this glorious road is a crossroads junction where you can turn left onto the Carrickmannon Road, following the signs for Raffrey and Killyleagh. This is another fine example of the Irish "B" road, and when I am on it, the reason the Irish Road Racing scene is the best in the world becomes clear. Dips are tunneled through trees and the field hedgerows dip right to the road side. I have always been acutely aware that if there is an accident on these roads it's going to hurt - the margin for error is nil, and that makes me feel alive.

The archaeology of the area is intriguing as there appears to be a lot packed into a relatively small area. Again the countryside is dotted with raths; however, there are published archaeological papers relating to a rath or fort and also an enclosure at Raffrey, although the site is now little more than collection of houses where the Carrickmannon Road becomes the Manse Road. The Northern Ireland Environment and Heritage site numbers for these are DOW016:021 and DOW016:022 respectively. Curiously, the first site is described as "Rath: the Fort" and the second enclosure as "Crannog: Dumb Lough". The Sites and Monuments Record (SMR) states that there is no lough remaining in the townland and it is possible that it has either naturally or by man's hand been drained. There appears to be some mystery as to where this site is actually located with the original article referring to a fort, and presumably ttis is why the SMR refers to the rath as the fort. But this is located on the edge of the bog and is therefore presumed to be the earthwork referred to in 1857. The reason the article was published was the discovery by a turf cutter of a cauldron, but the site clearly had some significance as:

> Other objects of antiquity have been found in the same vicinity, especially at a small lake called the "Dumb Lough" which adjoins the bog, and where numbers of warlike implements and some quern-stones were dug up. (MacAdam, 1857, 82).

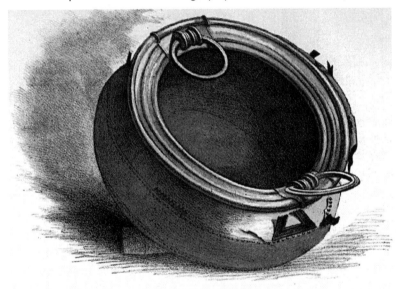

BRONZE CAULDRON,
found in the townland of Raffery, parish of Killinchy, Co. Down.

Drawing of the cauldron recovered from Raffrey (MacAdam, 1857, 83)

As with so many of these types of site, there are no remains to be seen, although to my knowledge the cauldron is complete and stored in the Ulster Museum.

The Manse Road can, if caught on the right day, be something of a lonely but satisfying ride. The long straights give way to

34

rising and sweeping crest turns that keep my mind occupied. It is on this type of road that I tend to let loose the thoughts caged within my head. It gives me time to think, and if you travel this same route it will no doubt have the same effect. The countryside, although tranquil in the summer, is fairly unremarkable and neutral, and so helps the mind flow into a meditative state. The negatives enter my head; the 'what if's' and the old mistakes that I have made ensure that regrets float though my head, gnawing viciously. The pain I have caused other people emerges from the muddy sludge of where I buried it in my subconscious, suddenly coming clear and into sharp focus. I wince at how uncomfortable it makes me. The Triumph acts like a comforting shoulder; warm, friendly and nonjudgmental and as I breathe deeply in and out, I attempt to flush everything out – after blinking hard my eyes reopen with renewed focus - the road is all I can now see - it's blackness carving through my misdeeds. This is why, for me, motorcycling is an almost spiritual experience; I know from asking other bikers that a few (although not all) also have these moments of fairly intense self doubt and exorcism.

The road is flanked by run-down vernacular houses and out buildings. Without any marker the Manse Road becomes the Clea Lough Road just after the Derryboye Cross Roads. The route I follow is straight, therefore there is no confusion at this junction. It is the sort of place I can imagine an Irish version of Robert Johnston meeting the Devil to gain insights into the blues! The road feels different somehow, although all that has really changed is the name. It seems more mature with indigenous trees like oak arching completely over the tarmac, and, when it's sunny, these majestic oaks provide much needed shade and welcome relief. Approximately three kilometres along this route, breaks in the hedge line give tantalizing glimpses of the body of water that the road is named after – on the left of the road is Clea Lough. It's a bit difficult to pull over as there is no verge or hard shoulder, but the landscape really opens up after passing over a stone bridge. This provides a fording at the point where the lough spills to the other side of the road. I have tried to find access points to the lough but have been unsuccessful; every point seems to be on someone's private land. This is a shame as the lake looks charming and could be classed as a beauty spot.

The hedges are also hiding more secrets, as the lough shore is packed with interesting sites, both on its fringes and on the water itself. I compiled an annotated aerial image to show just how many sites there are. It includes at least two crannogs, these are artificial lake islands used for human occupation or defense as well as being ceremonially significant. Also there are a cashel, a site named "The Hog's Mount" and another - a large circular feature visible from the air but not marked on the map.

The Ordnance Survey Maps are probably one of the most useful tools in initial research into the history of any area. The first two editions for this location clearly mark the area as having two distinct and separate bodies of water called Clay Lake North and Clay Lake South. It is only on the third edition (1857 – 1932) that the lake is represented as a single entity referred to as Clea Lakes. The first two editions refer to them as Clay Lakes.

> Clea Lough, also known as Clea Lakes, Killyleagh, Co. Down, most likely from the Irish Loch na Cléithe 'lake of the wattle', relating to Crannógs in the area. (NIPNP, 1987, 23).

An excavation was carried out on the crannog located on the eastern portion of the lake in 1956 by Collins and Proudfoot. This postdated an excavation undertaken by the landowner in the early 20th century that uncovered two bronze pins, a decorated stone disc and sherds of souterrain ware and medieval course ware. (Collins *et al,* 1959, 92). Souterrain ware has developmental stages, with simple plain sherds tending to date to the 7th – 8th centuries and the transition to more decorated pots pushing the date of some fragments to the end of the early medieval periods (Edwards, 1996, 74 – 75).

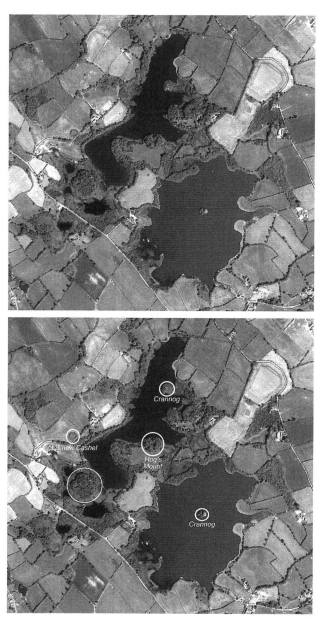

Aerial image (top) and annotated (bottom) of Clea Lough
(Bing Maps) © Microsoft Corporation

37

The 1956 excavation uncovered a plethora of finds that suggested an Early Christian date for the origin of the site.

> All the finds from the stratified deposit were probably pre-medieval in date...close dating of the finds is impossible but they are typical of the Early Christian or Dark Age period as a whole. (Collins *et al,* 1959, 94).

The site also revealed finds such as pins, a bead, bracelets fragments of quern stone, spindle whirls, worked flints as well as medieval pottery sherds, suggesting the crannog continued in use well into the medieval period. The appearance of the crannog was described by Fredengren:

> The crannog at Clea Lakes was supposedly surrounded by a stone wall which must have made it look like a cashel before it decayed. On the island were the remains of a stone building and a few hearths. (Fredengren, 2002, 53).

Neolithic pottery has also found on the lake shore suggesting that this part of the Strangford landscape has been use by humans for millennia.

On the western shore, approximately 150 metres from the shoreline and on gently sloping ground overlooking the water, is Lisinaw Cashel. I have found it spelt several different ways including Lisnaw, Lisinaw and Lislaw;

> The name is probably from the Irish *Lios an Átha* or fort of the ford. (NIPNP, 1987, 52).

The term cashel is mooted to be an Anglicised form of the Irish language word *Caiseal*, meaning castle and the sites are usually defined as circular stone walled enclosures.

The SMR dates the structure to the early Christian period and the Archaeological Survey of County Down describes the site as:

> ...a little over 100ft O.D on a rise overlooking Clea Lakes to the south east. It is about 110ft across and has a fairly massive wall built apparently entirely of stone, about 7ft thick. (ASCD, 1966, 178).

The 1993 Environment and Heritage Service survey describes it as:

> ...a well-preserved cashel surrounded by a dry-stone wall, tumbled in places with an entrance gap at the south east. The level, sheep-grazed interior measures 37 metres north – south by 35m east – west and slopes down to the south. Its average height is 1.2 metres. (SMR, 1993, DOW024:023).

The presence of the cashel, together with several crannogs suggests the whole lake area was of some significance and importance, either politically or ceremonially, maybe a local chieftain site, who knows?

Approximately one and a half kilometres south is a village that I didn't know existed until relatively recently – I took the road less travelled simply to explore and came upon Shrigley. The village reportedly grew up around the cotton mill and the stump of the mill chimney is still visible over the tree line from the Clea Lough Road.

> Shrigley is (or was) a small satellite industrial village about a mile north-west of Killyleagh. It grew up around the large six-storey cotton mill built in 1824 by John Martin; in 1836, Shrigley mill had more power looms than any other factory in Ireland ... The original mill was burned down in 1845; it was replaced by a flax-spinning mill, now occupied by United Chrometanners Limited. The Grecian gate pillars, and some of the subsidiary stone buildings, were probably survivors of the original mill, and stood until quite recently. (Brett, 1973, 8).

In the late 1960's / early 1970's the village was, in essence, wiped out and 'redeveloped'. Brett, writing in 1973, didn't mince his words describing the new housing estate-esque buildings he stated:

> ... they are laid out exactly like a suburban estate on the outskirts of a city. There is no variety, and there is no attempt to provide any kind of focus or heart to the community. There is not one element in the new estate which preserves or even recalls the identity of the old village. (*Ibid*).

I have to say I agree with him. The place feels souless and for that reason arouses in me a curious uneasy feeling; the history of the place is nothing more than a whisper on the light breeze that is completely failing to cool me in my leathers.

The Shrigley Monument or 'Martin Memorial' (Author)

I stopped at the Martin Monument, perhaps the last bastion of beauty in Shrigley, but even this was the subject of Brett's seething comments.

Only the Martin monument still stands, in isolation, at the mill gate: derelict, sprouting vegetation, with a number of its stones fallen, neglected, abandoned by the community which John

Martin created: in its present state, a decrepit eyesore. *Si monumentum requiris, circumspice* indeed! (*Ibid*).[2]

It is a shame as, if restored, the monument which originally functioned as a clock, lantern and drinking fountain, would add some beauty to a place where, for me, a lot of it has been cruelly ripped away. But it goes back to what I said earlier about the character of a lot of these small towns and villages being diluted then fading completely – an irreversible trend it seems.

As these thoughts crossed my mind, a curious face was peering at me from the factory. Like a child sheepishly pushing his luck, the owner gradually came over to admire the Tiger. He didn't give his name, at least I don't remember him doing so, but he instantly hunched down prodding at the engine and outlining why he thinks there are better bikes out there. I ground my teeth in annoyance. It is an aspect of biking that irritates me; everyone has their own preferences: their own style, bike type, riding gear, preferred engines etc. People should accept that rather than try to argue *their* way is the best way. Like so much in life, if we were all the same the world would be a very boring place!

I smoke a cigarette and make conversation about how hot it is on this mid-July day. The blue sky is an endless expanse above our heads and, despite the intrusion, I have a feeling of utter freedom that I want to savor.

I left Shrigley and headed roughly south east on the Shrigley Road towards Killyleagh. The whole road quickly became darker as the right side of the road is flanked with trees (presumably associated with Killyleagh Castle and its estate). The name of the town is thought to be from the Irish:

> ...*Cill Ó Laoch* from *Cin Lae Ó Mealláin* the 'church of the descendants of Laoch' the name is linked with the church ruins

---

[2]Roughly translated means, 'if you seek a monument, look around'.

1km north of village in the Townland Corporation. Anglicised references go back to 1306. (Muhr, 2008, DOW024:030).

On the Shrigley Road, a turn off to the right is marked by a brown sign saying 'Mary's Styles'. You can take this turn off as it leads to a gem – the semi-hidden ruins of Killowen Church; only after I started researching the site for this book did I realise its significance. I don't know why it is signposted the way it is, as I could not count the amount of times I have driven past it unaware of its existence.

The site is entered via a gateway crossing over a fairly fast flowing river. A neatly cut grass path leads towards the site passing over what appears to be a water-filled fosse – this could be a flooded original moat or boundary ditch. On the right, the gate opens to the tree enclosed church grounds. It feels private and away from humanity - not an unpleasing sensation. There are mounds that are firm under feet and perhaps contain rubble collapse from the church. Stumps of lichen blotched stones peep over the long grass and the whole site almost whistles when the wind blows.

Historically, there seem to be many references to the site, all with different names; Kilmeleyt (Killyleagh) is referred to in Pope Nicholas' taxation records (1306). Earlier forms of the name may be:

> Cell an laigh – the church of the hollow ... but the nearest seems to be Cell maghleth and we take leth to be the name of the river on which the church is situated. The present name of the church is Killowen – church of the river. (McKeown, 1934, 56 – 57).

O'Laverty tries to link a reference in the Annals of the Four Masters to the site:

> The Four Masters at the year 1149 speaking of the army led by Niall O'Loughlin say…Cill-Aedhain, pronounced Kill-een, presents in sound a great similarity to Killowen, the position of which would correspond with the account in the Annals. (O'Laverty, 1878, 331 – 332).

42

For me, this is maybe a little tenuous. Although it is possible there was some form of religious site there before the 13th century, it seems likely that the church site was built or at least developed in association with the motte site erected by John de Courcy in the late 12th – 13th centuries.

The remains currently there may be slightly later. The papal grant in 1513 makes no mention of the site, suggesting it was already in ruin by that stage. Its redevelopment and repair seems to coincide with the building of part of the current castle in Killyleagh in the mid 1600's. However, fragments of stone decorated in the Romanesque style were recovered from the site, this style dates to the 12th – 13th centuries, which I think confirms my personal hypothesis of a de Courcy date for the original church. However, no doubt an academic somewhere is scoffing in their wooly jumper or elbow patches at this theory! Interesting carved stones were also recorded from the site in the 1800's.

The Romanesque carved stone (Waterman, 1971, Plate XXIII)

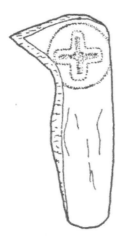
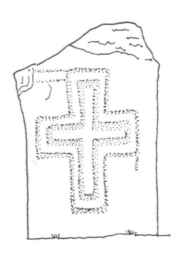

Drawings of the carved stones found at Killowen Church (Patterson, 1879, 273 – 276)

Ruins at Killowen Church (Author)

44

View of the ruins at Killowen Church and burial ground (Author)

Killyleagh Castle is across the road from Killowen and is hard to miss as is looms over the village. It is supposed to be based architecturally on a Loire-style chateau. Although I have stopped at it frequently for a breather and cigarette, for me it is a little Disney-esque and over the top. The castle is recorded as a multi-period castle on the site of the earlier motte. The current structure is much later with the turrets added in the 1800's but the core remains from the mid 1600's.

On one such stop there was a family having a picnic in front of the gatehouse, the small boy's face lit up when I arrived on the bike, wide-eyed he came over to see the machine. His dad was behind and began chatting to me admiringly. I told him to lift his son onto the seat and duly started the bike up; my foot carefully covering the gear lever so that he couldn't accidently put the bike in gear. I have seen that happen with my friend's bike. Someone claiming to know all about bikes was sitting on his Kwak and flicked the bike into first gear, it careered forward catapulting the 'rider' off and hit a wall, destroying the front forks. I was mindful not to have a repeat incident with a

45

child on board! I told him to gently ease the throttle back and instead he revved the bike up to the redline! If nothing else, it certainly would have cleared the pipes!

Killyleagh Castle gatehouse (Author)

Once through Killyleagh the road widens to become an 'A' road, the A22 Downpatrick Road heading roughly south-west. I have always enjoyed this road as it is in exceptional condition and has a race track feel to it, although *please don't* take this as a green light by me or anyone else to treat it as one, even though some of the corners resemble *eau rouge* at Spa! As the bike tilts over, in places plunging through the trees that the road cuts through, the sense of speed increases and the thrill rate with it. The one drawback is that it can be fairly busy, but the long straights enable overtaking with ease, with the gentle, somehow strolling, drumlin countryside providing green streaks in my peripheral vision.

Approximately five kilometres along this road is a right turning marked by a sign for Derryboye. The road forks immediately after this turn off. You should take the left fork onto the

Greystown Road. The tarmac surface is rougher, more stony, and as soon as the middle road markings disappear the road narrows. It continues to do so until it becomes little more than a tarmac laneway just metres wide. The hedgerows are tall and encroach from above, providing a wall of green on either side, even on a sunny day, making it feel cooler. The straights are punctuated with sweeping blind corners and on the occasions when there is a brief break in the hedgerows, it feels like coming up from under water, desperate for a gasp of air before diving back down again into a green sea.

In autumn, the colours are kaleidoscopic; with yellow, red and brown hues and the roadway itself like a leaf carpet. The tunnel vision I develop on this road consumes everything else; no other thoughts enter my head. I have a clarity of focus, with my senses heightened due to the potential danger the road presents, given even a momentary slip in concentration. The hedges give way to more open fields; the palpable sense of relief is all too brief before the trees overarch the road again. The Greystown Road ends at the junction with the A7 Belfast Road and allows the rider to reduce concentration levels slightly. Here you should turn left, and, after a leisurely cruise on this unremarkable road for approximately one and half kilometres, there is a right turning marked by a brown sign for Inch Abbey – take this turning onto the Inch Abbey Road. Once on this I feel as though I have been transported to some medieval fantasy landscape. Although there is nothing to give this impression, it's just how the road makes me feel. Just over five hundred metres along this avenue is a left turn off, marked by the characteristic Environment and Heritage service green gates. If you travel up this hill, park up and for a moment take in the breathtaking scene. Situated in, for what in the modern world is splendid isolation, are the remains of Inch Abbey.

Before I go into detail about the site I should explain what this place means to me, for it means an awful lot and occupies a special place in my soul. On more than one occasion I have found myself here to think, re-evaluate and process what has happened in my life. As a result I am weirdly selfish about it. I do not like it when other people are there. I want it to myself. It's as if the place speaks to me and I do not want that polluted by 'Sunday drivers'. I find the setting lends itself to quiet reflection and frequently find that I have much to reflect upon, wrestling with my inner demons. I find myself wondering if other people have sat in the same spot, either recently or centuries ago, working through the same or similar problems. I guess one of the things I learned recently from my Dad is that you may think your problems are unique, but they aren't! Someone, somewhere has been through it all before and got the t-shirt long before you. If all the world's troubles were in a barrel ... you'd soon reach back in for your own! When I have the site to myself, I am convinced the solutions to my problems present themselves as if through the spirits of those once there. When the ruins 'talk' to me they provide clarity. Inch is also one of the first destinations I took my other half to when she was first learning to ride pillion.

There is a long history to the site. The name Inch is derived from *Inis Cúscraidh* 'island or water-meadow' and although Inch currently provides a fine example of a Cistercian Abbey which was founded by John de Courcy in 1187 (ASCD, 1966, 279), it has been demonstrated that a church had existed here for two centuries before de Courcy's time:

> ...its real name was *Inis Cumhscraidh* (in fact, the presence of a much earlier church is indicated by a reference *to Inis Cúscraid* as early as c.830 in the Martyrology of Oengus. It is asserted in the epic tale *Táin Bo Cuailnge* or 'The Cattle Raid of Cooley' that it was once inhabited by *Cúscraidh Mend Macha*, son of *Conchobar*, king of Ulster, whose seat was at *Emain Macha*, now Navan Fort in Co. Armagh. (http://www.placenamesni.org/).

The Annals of Tigernach record:

> Sitriuc son of Olaf, king of the Foreigners went in his galleys on a foray into Ulster, and he plundered *Cell Cleithe* and *Inis Cumscraig*, and carried out of them many captive. (MacNiociall, 2010, 355).

48

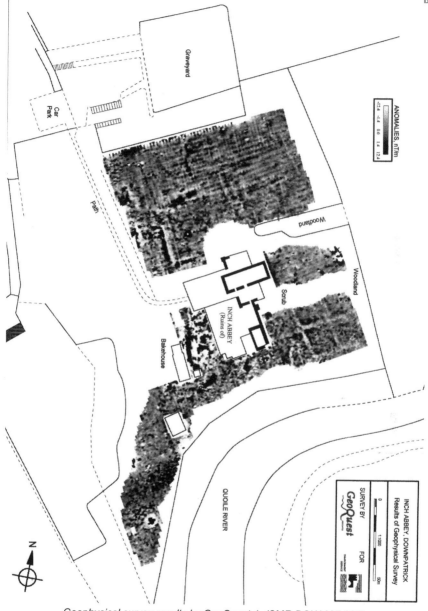

Geophysical survey results by GeoQuest,1 (SMR DOW 037:005)

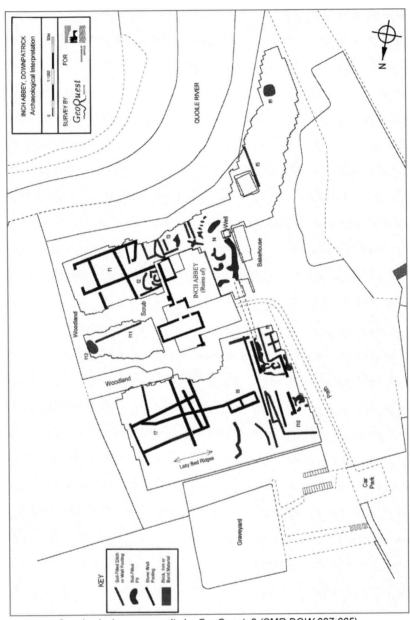

Geophysical survey results by GeoQuest, 2 (SMR DOW 037:005)

50

Inis Cumscraig is, presumably, a variation of *Inis Cumhscraidh.* The Norse sounding names of the 'foreigners' refer to Viking raids on the religious site.

Given that the site is on earlier probably monastic remains, a geophysical survey was carried out by GeoQuest in 2001 with interesting results. It showed a superfluity of what appeared to be walls and other covered features on the site. Right under foot, as one stands and looks at the magnificent remains that are there today, are the ghosts of the earlier buildings.

I genuinely believe that there are spiritual places. It doesn't necessarily follow that there has been a prehistoric ceremonial site or early Christian site on the land, for me there are areas that just seem to exude a presence. Inch is one of those places. Looking east across the Quoile River the Mound of Down is visible in the near distance. The urban sprawl of Downpatrick seems to be like some kind of untidy grey accident against the ritual landscape.

I like to run my hands over the stonework, wander through the buildings and look up to the exquisite gothic pointed arch windows and imagine that it had the same, probably even more powerful, effect on someone standing there almost a thousand years earlier. You do not have to be faithful in order to be spiritual at Inch. She forgives all.

The reconstruction drawings of the whole complex are impressive and make it obvious that these sites were more than simply churches in various places. They were also important social and political centres strategically positioned in the landscape.

More recently, the site, along with others along this route such as Castle Ward and Walshestown, has been used as a film set for HBO's epic and enjoyable series 'Game of Thrones'.

On leaving the site, you can return to the main A7 Belfast Road and turn right towards Downpatrick. The roundabout into

Inch Abbey looking roughly north-east (Author)

Inch Abbey looking east (Author)

52

the town is only a short distance. Take the second exit towards the town centre and onto Church Street where road veers to the right up a gentle slope. This is Bridge Street and there are brown signs for the Cathedral and Mound of Down. There is also a pub with a large Guinness symbol painted on the gable which can act as a guide. The hill is bordered on either side by 60's styled small houses, but as the Cathedral tower looms into view there is a turn off for a small laneway to the right. This is a downslope to the epic Mound of Down.

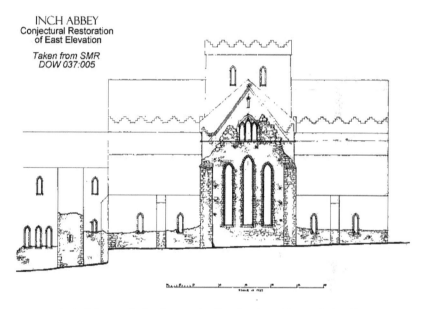

*Inch Abbey conjectural reconstruction drawing of the east elevation
(Environment and Heritage Service: Sites and Monuments Record – DOW037:005)*

The Mound of Down is exceptionally imposing which was, after all, the intention in its construction. Like Navan Fort in Armagh there is a tangible sense of history here. It is as if it stretches back, not only physically into time, but also into mythology. Digging into the history of the site can get complicated, but physically it consists of a large oval earthwork surrounded by a massive bank and ditch and a

53

circular mound which rises from the interior of the platform. It was probably reused later as an unfinished motte.

The oval enclosure is most likely an earlier site, possibly an Iron Age hill fort reused as a bailey by the Normans. The mound measures 54 metres by 55 metres in diameter and is 12.5 metres high and separated from the bailey by a ditch with a causeway at the south west. The oval enclosure is 215 metres by 167 metres. (SMR, DOW037:028). The Norman elements - the motte and potential bailey - were built by John de Courcy after his defeat of Rory Mac Donlevy (or MacDunlevy) in 1177.

The name for the site is reported as taken from the Irish *Ráth Cealtchair* meaning 'Cealtchar's rath' and it is also referred to as '*Celtchar's fort*' in a De Courcy charter in 1200. *Cealtchar* (or *Celtchar mac Uthidir*) was a hero in the Irish tales and taken to be a local chieftain. (NIPNP, 1987, 68). The *Táin* describes him as:

> ...a worthy adversary. He is a hero in prowess. He is [like] a stormy wave which overwhelms. He is [like] the sea pouring across boundaries. That was Celtchair mac Cuithechair from Dún Lethglaise in the north. (O'Rahilly, C., 1976, 226).

Dún Lethglaise in the *Táin Bó Cúalnge* is described as his dwelling. This later varies to 'Downpatrick' and presumably also refers to the Mound of Down.

I can imagine him, whether mythical or real is immaterial. He was the sort of man that doesn't seem to exist anymore, like a giant amongst other men. The pre-Norman site is also reputed to be a likely royal stronghold of the *Dál Fiatach*, the clan that ruled this part of County Down in the first millennium AD. It seems to have become the administrative centre of the Kings of *Dál Fiatach* by the early Christian period (Stewart, 2012). Lawlor writing in 1919 – 1920 disagrees with some of the historical analysis, stating that the site is known as the English Mount or '*Donecoscue*' and that his excavations suggest that it was not the site of an ancient settlement and therefore cannot be *Rathkeltchar* (Lawlor, 1919, 144). The eminent

54

castle expert Dr Tom McNeill does concur with there being an earlier Gaelic site before its reuse as a Norman fortification, suggesting that there are problems with attributing the whole site and its initial construction to the Anglo-Normans and he concludes that:

> ... the earthwork must be attributed to MacDunlevy before 1177 with an attempted fortification by the Anglo-Normans, abandoned before it was finished. (McNeill, 1980, 13).

Aerial image of the Mound of Down (Image taken by and used with kind permission of Gavin Donaghy of Irish Archaeological Research Ltd.)

Whatever the historical source-based inconsistencies, de Courcy took *Dún Dá Leathghlas* (Downpatrick) and after his defeat of the Irish in 1177 his power spread ever further; the old Irish kingdoms of *Oriel* and *Ulaidh* or *Ulidia* disappeared, fading into annals and mythical memory. The Annals of Ulster state:

> Dun-da-lethglas was destroyed by John De Courcy and by the knights that came with him, and a castle was made by them there, wherefrom they twice inflicted defeat upon Ulidia and defeat upon Cenel-Eoghain and upon Airgialla; where was killed Conchobur Ua Cairella. (Bambury *et al*, 2000, 185).

The Annals of the Four Masters outline his dominance as reaching even further:

> ... An army was led by John De Courcy and the knights into Dalaradia and to Dun da leathghlas; they slew Donnell, the grandson of Cathasach, Lord of Dalaradia. Dun da leathghlas was plundered and destroyed by John and the knights who came in his army. (Hondelink, 2002, 30 – 31).

There are plenty of places around the mound to sit in quiet contemplation; the advantage of its size is that it is always possible to find some 'alone' space. The 'vibe' the place creates is sublime.

I had parked the bike in the shade in the parking bay but it and everything else seemed so far away. The mound felt as if it were in the middle of the countryside but alas the sounds from the town pierce the silence, reminding me of my true location. The trees act as a shield no longer. I imagine the battles here: the warriors and heroes of Irish myth – how or what would I have been if I had been alive back then? The bike calls from afar - she tells me it's time to go.

There are a myriad of ways out of Downpatrick but the advisable route to take is for the B1 Ardglass Road. It lies to the south of the town approached from Irish Street, Edward Street or John Street. At the junction of the Ardglass Road and Ballyhornan Road, the traveller has a choice: there are signposts to Struell Wells that take the Ardglass Road route or one can carry on the Ballyhornan Road, taking the right turn onto the Struell Wells Road. This is an easy road to miss but is more rewarding, as it reverts to a narrow ribbon of tarmac laneway through the countryside. It is quiet and tranquil - the reverberation of the engine noise off the stone field walls and trees the only company anyone could need. One passes old stone built barns with corrugated metal roofing.

When I take this route, I trail brake the bike into the corners, noticing the trees when they have no foliage are gnawed and wizened like old ogres trying to discourage my progress, but they fail. Beside a rather grand house is a right turning, marked by one of the ubiquitous brown signs, for Struell Wells.

The road has trees on the right and a small stonewall to the left. The ground slopes downwards and away from the entrance on the left, roughly north east. On approaching the site it seems quite sparse and open, only later is it apparent how many smaller buildings there are; odd structures resembling out houses that are the eye well and another the drinking well. The eye wells are interesting as they were used by pilgrims to bathe the eyes; the holy waters were believed to relieve physiological conditions, although whether the bathing was more ritualistic than practical, as is the case with the Islamic practice of washing before prayer, is open to debate.

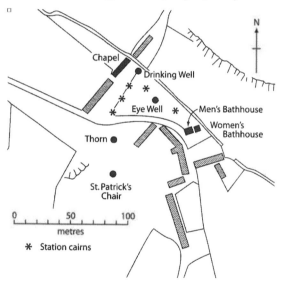

Plan of Struell Wells with the published annotations (McCormick, 2009, 1)

Small rocks protrude from the ground and one sees a larger windowed building that is the later chapel. If one continues past the car parking area further down the lane, past two buildings associated with the site that are the men's and woman's bath houses, there lies a ghostly vernacular house. It must have been a strange yet interesting place to live. The open rock face behind the site initially gives the appearance that the place was hewn out of the solid rock, giving a feeling of solidity. In reality it probably provided the building materials.

The name Stuell is thought to come from the *An tSruthail* or 'the stream' (NIPNP, 1987, 80) the site is therefore presumably named for the reason it was placed there. The site is referred to in the eighth century, but the references to its healing powers are eleventh or twelfth century in date;

> ...the site continued to be a focus of pilgrimage at midsummer until its suppression in the nineteenth century. (McCormick, 2009, 1).

McCormick's account of why the site was significant is also intriguing:

> What sets Struell apart from any other place of pilgrimage in Ireland, or elsewhere, is the naked bathing that occurred at the site. The records indicate that the purpose of the bathing was to cure illnesses and to protect health in the future. Lady Elizabeth Cromwell had tried to separate the sexes with the building of the Men's Bathhouse, but this segregation had disappeared by the nineteenth century. Use of the Men's Bathhouse was confined to those who could afford to pay for the privacy it provided. *(Ibid, 55).*

The place sounds relatively raucous and good fun:

> In the evenings those attending appear to have indulged in more secular activities, which no doubt contributed to the attractions of the pilgrimage: 'In [the] tents, and in the adjoining fields, under the canopy of a pure sky, they spend the whole night, quaffing the soul-inspiring beverage, and indulging in various gratifications to which the time and place are favourable. (*Ibid*).

This seems to be a complete contradiction to what I always imagined a pilgrim to do; then again in recent years my Dad has completed the pilgrimage trail of the *Camino de Santiago*, to the church of Santiago de Compostela in Spain, quite a few times completely on foot, staying at small hostels along the route. The tales of drinking gallons of rioja and general *craic* are awesome; once or twice he has gone on a whim on his own and made new friends there - not bad for a man in his 70's! I suppose what happened at Struell was quite similar, the pilgrimage was probably a journey that created bonds and friendship.

To continue on our own journey, once out of the Struell site, you may continue along the Struell Wells Road. There are undulating long straights with low hedgerows in places where it is possible to take in and enjoy the countryside. For myself, that light and airy feeling returns to the space within my helmet. I don't know why, but despite ample opportunity to twist the throttle I tend to meander along this road; maybe the spiritual sites have had an effect and rendered a more serene state of mind, or maybe I'm just tired of mulling over the things I cannot change. *Nihil Poeniteat*[3] - easier said than done!

At the end of the Struell Wells Road is a junction where it rejoins the Ballyhornan Road. You could turn right here to rejoin the road. The Ballyhornan Road is, in my opinion, one of the nicest motorbike roads you will find – asphalt heaven! Just over a kilometre along this road is a small hamlet and just beyond this the road forks. Take the left turn following the signs for Lough Money; this is now the Ballyculter Road. Be wary on this road, as the dips can flood with even mild rainfall and farm vehicles can drag a lot of mud and stones onto the surface. The road appears to fork. although the right turn is, as far as I can make out, private. On the right hand side is a small overgrown mound almost directly due south of Lough Money and is of some significance – Ballyalton Court Cairn.

The site is Neolithic (stone age) in date but the finds included human bones from several individuals, flint artifacts (arrowheads, knives and axes), and pottery sherds (SMR, 1995, DOW038:006).

---

[3] Regret nothing.

Ballyhornan Road (Tele Atlas, 2009 © Google Maps)

The site is referred to in many ways: Druidical Ring, Horned Cairn, Court Tomb, Court Cairn, Chambered Court Cairn and Megalith. Although overgrown, the site can still be accessed. It was excavated and an account published in 1934, outlining the discovery of an oval cairn aligned north-west by south-east with the cairn covering the megalith slab stones. Along the main body of the monument was a gallery of long shale slabs which were segmented into distinct chambers (SMR, 1995, DOW038:006). When they were excavated, it was found that the site, from the portal stones at the entrance, measured 75ft (22.8 metres) in length by 65ft (19.1 metres) in width. The chambers themselves being 25ft (7.68 metres) with a roughly paved floor surface. (Evans *et al, 1934,* 81).

The following description might be a bit technical, but I think worthwhile, as it shows the significance of some of the discoveries made around the lough. The pottery sherds uncovered during the excavation were noteworthy as they were a type of well made vertical linear grooved and whipped cord decorated Neolithic pottery, dating to the late 4th and early 3rd millennia BC. But they are a distinct type of their own and known as the 'Ballyalton Bowls'. (Darvill, 2008).

60

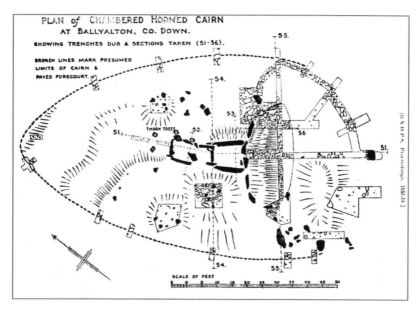

PLAN of CHAMBERED HORNED CAIRN
AT BALLYALTON, Co. DOWN.
SHOWING TRENCHES DUG & SECTIONS TAKEN (51-56).

BROKEN LINES MARK PRESUMED
LIMITS OF CAIRN &
PAVED FORECOURT.

Plan of Ballyalton (Evans et al, 1934)

The significance of the landscape as a whole is highlighted by a few prehistoric monuments in close proximity. To the north lies Slievenagriddle portal tomb (DOW038:015), which on a clear day has views to the Irish Sea, Isle of Man and even Cumbria. To the west can be seen the Mournes and to the north-east is Loughmoney portal tomb (DOW031:002), which is located close to Carrownacaw standing stone (the Long Stone: DOW031:001). Also nearby are the Castlemahon stone circle and cist cremation burial (DOW 031:022) and Castlemahon enclosure (DOW031:063). It is clear, given the sheer number of sites, that during the Neolithic this area was important, with burials, cremations and standing stones. The well-worn term 'ritual site' is as usual carted out and applied, but I think it is probably apt.

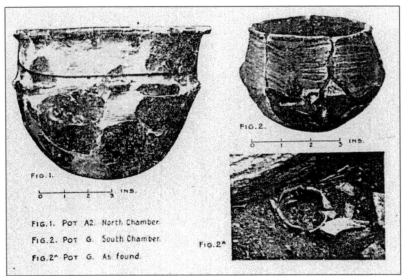

Ballyalton Bowls (Evans et al, 1934, Plate IV)

The route I like to take flanks the east side of Lough Money, but you can easily visit these other sites, as I have done, as they are so close to the road and easily accessible. When you are on higher ground you get a sense of why the landscape might have been important. Not only are the views spectacular but it is an area that exudes something akin to what I talked about earlier, a lineage somehow to our ancestors and their beliefs. It's as if their spiritual selves remain, whispering in the ear the importance of where one is standing. The wind on the exposed higher ground, even on an otherwise still day, can be quite strong, adding to the atmosphere. The roads amble their way over the drumlins and are satisfying as a result.

Lough Money is a derivative from the Irish *Loch Móna* or 'lough of the bog' (NIPNP, 1987, 53). Now the lough is an angling fishery with trout restocked each year, it is also a destination for 'wild swimming' and Maureen McCoy's account of swimming in the lough is almost poetic:

> The Lough is picturesque with water lilies just beginning to bloom when we arrive. It stretches north, approximately 1 km long and fairly narrow …The temperature was very pleasant, as

soon as I glided off into the Lough it felt beautiful, a temperature where I knew I could take my time, stop for a chat and enjoy the view...The rain began in earnest. It's a lovely thing to swim in the rain, the surface of the water softened, broken by the raindrops, seeing the tiny splashes each time you turn and breathe, feeling the cool rain on your arms as you take each stroke. (wildswim.wordpress.com/2013/05/10/lough-money-co-down/).

She is brave, but despite her picturesque account, I don't know if I could do that. I have body-boarded off White Rocks (Portrush) in the middle of December, although that was in a 5mm wetsuit and the water temperature was warmer than the ambient air temperature. The snow was falling and hissing as it hit the reference fire lit on the beach – the presence of hallucinogens in my blood stream making it even more exhilarating, if a foolhardy and irresponsible experience. Those days are, I hasten to add, long, long gone! The folly of youth perhaps a reason, but not an excuse for such experimentation.

Once past the junction with the Ballyculter Road, heading roughly north, the Loughmoney Road runs to the west of the lough and is sunken as if ancient and hewn from the countryside. A steep grass bank is on the right hand side in the main, and is situated on the right side of the road once past the farms. The road surface is old and tired, the pits and pot-holes hidden by puddles. The thud that reverberates up the forks from the front tyre and suspension force a sharp intake of breath; the fear that I might have damaged something all the more poignant as it is a distinct possibility. The bike has registered her displeasure! The grass bank[s] are punctuated with low drystone walls, white with age and weathering. I always think the weathering is like grey hair, somehow an indicator of age and wisdom. Looking west, to the left, the countryside opens to rolling hills and at the right time of year crops such as maze have dried and their leaves almost crackle in the wind. The road isn't used much, the most frequent vehicle on it is usually a piece of farm machinery, so beware of tractors and the mud on the roads. I have frequently had the back-end slide and have had to be careful not to over correct in order to avoid a 'tank slapper' as I powered into the slide.

The road seems to ramble across the countryside in an organic fashion, in sympathy with the landscape. Somehow the mud dragged across it acts almost as a camouflage, making it blend in with the surroundings. There are many small junctions along this road and the route I take is straight towards Raholp, not taking any turnoffs, but my advice is to explore this countryside as it isn't busy or much used by the casual tourist.

Approximately five hundred metres before the road ends in a T-junction, there are ruined vernacular buildings flanking both sides of the road, each with a thicket of trees growing out of them. Nature is reclaiming them and it won't be long before she is victorious! At the T-junction you might want to turn left and head west onto the St. Patrick's Road towards Saul. There is a ruined church and early Christian site at Raholp located of the Bannaghan Road to the east. The site consists of a reconstructed rectangular church on top of a plinth in the field. An excavation was carried out there by the Centre for Archaeological Fieldwork in 2003. The village itself is, though, little more than a residential hamlet.

The St. Patrick's Road is only slightly wider than the Loughmoney Road, but the slight increase makes all the difference to one's perception. The road surface is also newer and yields more grip. The road opens to more straights and the line of vision is much further, giving me increased confidence and a renewed impetus. Eventually the road begins to sweep downhill towards Saul, with the off-camber corners adding an additional but fun extra dimension to this part of the ride. The road becomes Mearne Road and enters a residential area with houses on both sides. You can continue until the road forks then keep straight (veering slightly right) to continue along the Mearne Road. The direction is marked by a yellow coloured building - Paddy's Barn - an inviting looking pub and restaurant; the sort in which I can imagine nursing a

64

pint of Guinness in front of the fire on a cold winters evening. Immediately past this, the road narrows and taller trees border both sides of the road. An eerie and dilapidated vernacular house is on the left, situated right in eye-line on a left hand kink. The road rises and the trees thin until arriving at a junction. Here you can turn left onto the Saul Road following the brown arrow sign for Saul Church.

The name Saul is from Irish *Sabhall* or 'barn, barn-shaped church' and it is named for both the early life of St Patrick, *Sabul Patricii* or 'Patrick's Saul' and his burial place *sepulturam Patrici* (Muhr, 2008). The church site is originally early Christian in date and for those interested in the life of Ireland's patron saint, quite important. The church here has an association with St. Patrick's mission to Ireland in the 5th Century. It is referred to in the 7th century and later annals as the place of his death (ASCD, 1966, 287). The church is recorded as being founded in 432AD, over one and a half thousand years ago and perhaps an indication as to why the village got its name:

> There was a barn in the place, which the hero Díchu gave to the holy Patrick, and he desired that the house of God should be built towards the sun, after the form of his barn. (O'Laverty, 1878, 229).

The Annals of the Four Masters record an attack on the site in 1170 by the then King of *Ulidia* and a monk called *Amliamh* or *Amhlaeibh*. He was deposed of his abbacy by monks from Mellifont.

> An unknown, atrocious deed was committed by *Maghnus Ua hEochadha*, King of *Ulidia*, and the monk *Amhlaeibh*, son of the successor of *Finnen*, and by the *Ulidians* in general ... a convent of religious monks, with their abbot, whom *Maelmaedhog Ua Morgair* legate of the successor of Peter, had appointed at *Sabhall-Phadraig* [Saul Patrick or Patrick's Saul] were expelled from the monastery which they themselves had founded and erected; and they were all plundered both of their books and ecclesiastical furniture. (Hondelink, 2002, 1181).

The site now consists of a modern 'interpretation' of an early Christian church, but the gable end of what appears to be a medieval church building is still visible in the enclosure.

I have to say when you first arrive at the site and peer down the avenue of trees, the modern church 'styled' on an early church looks so Disney and fake you almost want to get straight back on the bike. I know that there are some buildings that are deliberately like this, to ensure there is no confusion with other remains, but even in this context this seems to have gone a little too far. There are records of early cross inscribed slabs and headstones as well as stone lined graves that contained white pebbles and even a souterrain at the site. (SMR, 2004, DOW031:042). The stone lined graves (cists) are perhaps an indication of early Christian date burials, where the actual hole dug to contain the body was lined with stone as an *in situ* coffin of sorts. The carved stones and slabs from the site are outlined in the Sites and Monument Record and also recorded by Patterson and published in 1892.

Carved stone at Saul, 1 (Patterson, 1892, 433)

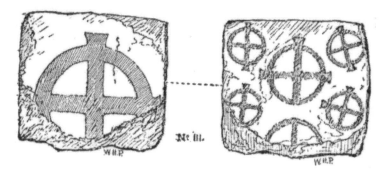

Carved stone at Saul, 2 (SMR – DOW031:042)

I was gloriously alone on the site, the feint hums of insects a welcome distraction as they darted to wild meadow flowers and this took the edge of my single raised eyebrow at the modern church in front of me.

The Triumph at the entrance gate to Saul showing the tree lined avenue (Author)

The medieval wall remains at Saul (Author)

Immediately to the left of the church is where the site, for me, becomes intriguing. The single masonry wall stands like some megalith, solitary and seemingly out of place, but it is undoubtedly the remains of a medieval structure. The small mortuary house is clearly visible on the site; the purpose of these buildings has caused some debate among academics. Other examples of similar buildings were used to house burials, other supposed mortuary houses have been used as small spaces for confession, personal devotion or as repositories for artifacts and relics. The site has been left to overgrow slightly between the early headstones and carved stones, although I like the juxtaposition of this wilder area and the tight clipped grass around the church. As I walked towards the mortuary house the sense of intrigue is heightened by its appearance, which gives no clues as to what one might find inside, the uneven ground invisible beneath the long grass that almost makes me lose my footing. It creates a sense of nervousness somehow - the uncertainty of its function combined with the somewhat challenging walk to its small entrance arouses my curiosity. The small upstanding stones, presumably early headstones and remnants, protrude only slightly above the grass, at times appearing like a spine directing me towards the mortuary house. I run my hands along the top of the wild grasses that look soft, but as I soon discover are quite 'bristly' and barbed; not in a painful way, but not as I expected.

In truth there isn't really much to see other than the structure. Inside this it is overgrown and fairly nondescript but it does feel ancient. I don't know if it was the presence of the modern church behind me or just the sort of day that I visited, the site seemed devoid of a spiritual essence, especially when compared with Nendrum, Tullynakill, Inch Abbey and the like. I find the site really interesting but it fails to move me.

The Mortuary House at Saul (Author)

Located to the west of the complex on top of a hill called Slieve Patrick (*Shliabh Phádraig*) is a large granite stature of the saint. In my opinion, the statue is hideous as he looms over the countryside like a soldier and tyrant rather than a saint, but each to their own.

After leaving the church you can travel north down the hill, turning left onto the Mearne Road. Incidently, the name Mearne Road (*Bóthar na Teorann*) is taken from the Anglisation of 'Mearne Well' but the origin is a bastardization of *Tobar Phádraig* which means St. Patrick's Well.

> The well is to be found on the boundary with Quoile, Inch, and is also a parish boundary, a fact which gives rise to its English name as 'Mearne' would seem to be a corruption of the English word mearing. (NIPNP, 1987, 57).

I have been on this road countless times and it has always been simply a strip of tarmac to get to somewhere else. It is a nice road but there is no feeling associated with it. Oddly enough I have a tendency to have a 'brain fart' on this little section and zone out what is around me in a daydream.

When you reach the junction with the A25 Strangford Road it is advisable to turn right, following the signs for Strangford. For me this has always been a beautiful road and I am snapped out of my trance. The road is flanked on the left by trees and the Quoile River. The river banks have lovely walks amongst the trees and, if time allows, I advise stopping, getting out of the bike gear, relaxing for an hour or two and maybe have a picnic as there are ample places to do so. Walking along the river's edge roughly north-east as it gets wider and closer to the main lough, you will find the number of people tends to thin out – always a good thing! There are stretches of reed beds from the shore, their white wispy tops swaying in the breeze and in autumn they add a golden colour to the river.

Approximately four hundred metres from the Mearne Road junction, the glorious Strangford Road veers round an almost 90 degree right turn corner, but instead of taking this bend, carry straight on to the Quay Road, following the brown sign for the Quoile Countryside Centre. Approximately three hundred metres along this road it is nigh impossible to miss the tower stump of Quoile Castle and the Countryside Centre in the grounds.

Quoile Castle showing the collapsed section (Author)

I presume the castle takes its name after the Quoile River which is from the Irish *An Caol* 'the narrow [water]' (NIPNP, 1987, 66). The river was tidal until 1957 / 1958 when a barrier was built at Castle Island by the Ministry of Agriculture. When first built, the castle would have been surrounded on two sides by tidal water and the Spring Tide would have come right up to the walls (Ó Baoill, 2011, 7). Architectural details have conventionally been used to date the castle to the late 16th century, but Ó Baoill notes that the structure is not on any 16th century maps, although late-Elizabethan silver sixpences (the latest dating from 1593) found during conservation works does seem to corroborate the late 16th century construction (*Ibid*, 4). The castle was once more complete as it was, after all, still lived in perhaps into the 19th century. But just like Sketrick Castle, a major section of the wall collapsed, leaving the form you see today, even though it was repaired in the late 1970's.

For me the castle is a little odd; there are houses and gardens right up against it as well as the Countryside Centre. For that reason, and the new looking pointing, it looks almost like a garden feature or folly rather than castle. However, it gives a quaint feel to the whole site. On entering the castle immediately to my right are found the stairs. The first floor is open with the stairs to what would have been the higher levels barred by a gate. Back on the ground floor there are two vaulted rooms, the second dimmer than the first so, I have to squint to get my eyes used to the gloom. There was a slightly damp smell from the masonry that is not unpleasing, but in sharp contrast to the heat and dry grass outside. For some reason I have a desire to linger, the location is peaceful and calming, so it's easy to relax.

There is a grass bank near the castle and it seems to be angled perfectly for lying on, so I took off my jacket and the weight off my back. I couldn't help my eyes slowly closing as the heat from the sun warmed my face. I was even more comfortable with one arm behind my head as a pillow. Gusts of wind rustled the long grasses and reeds near the river producing a very comforting sound. The noise of a family at one of the picnic tables for once does not annoy me; their laughter muffled by the large weeping willow between us; its lower branches gently scraping of the ground. All the sounds become a murmur on the breeze. After a long bike ride the spiritual element of the journey is more potent.

My parents tried to plant a willow in our old back garden, it never got anywhere near the height of the one at Quoile, but I like their form; the small furry buds feel nice rubbed between my thumb and forefinger. I am instantly transported back to childhood - how I wish I could go back. Knowing what I know now, I would do things differently.

72

The Countryside Centre has photo points around the site to capture images of the wildlife and the elongated stone building would make a lovely cottage. The garden in front is planted and a helpful grid pattern shows how to maximize the space to grow your own fruit and veg.

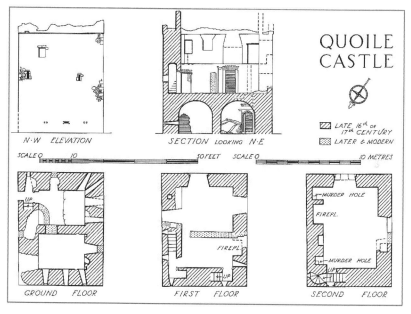

Elevation and plan drawings of Quoile Castle (ASCD, 1966, 247)

The Quay Road continues roughly north-east becoming a narrow laneway encroached by what appears to be every tree type possible in the Irish climate. Autumn is an astounding sight and the ideal time of year to take this route, as the colours of the leaves are spectacular. Although the lane is a dead end, it leads to a car parking area overlooking a wide section of the Quoile River, with a slope covered in trees reaching down to the water's edge on the other bank. In the summer of 2013 when I took this route for the first time, an old man frantically flagged me down.

I stopped and lifted my visor; "You need to slow down there, boy!" This confused me as I wasn't going fast. "It's because there's a wedding photo shoot and they have horses - they might bolt".

It all made sense. I turned the bike off and dismounted "That's a lovely machine you've got, ideal weather for it too." He wasn't wrong! I sauntered down to the car park area and sure enough there were some beautiful horses, their big eyelashes attempting to get flies away from their eyes. I asked the handler if I could stroke them, "Knock yourself out! it'll be a good ten or fifteen minutes before we're taking pictures". I rubbed the nose of a chestnut brown horse, its eyes half closing in what I presume was satisfaction as I did so, or maybe it just gave up trying to 'blink' the flies away.

The road from the site rejoins the A25 Strangford Road. I think it is this road that comes to mind for most bikers when they think of an ideal location to ride; it has tight twists, sweeping full-throttle corners and long straights, all with a silky smooth surface. All this, however, means flies get in ones teeth! In places the trees arch from both sides of the road to completely enclose it in a green tunnel. Small birds play dare with the front tyre between the hedgerows.

Approximately one and a half kilometres from the Quoile turn-off is a left turn onto the Lisboy Road; I haven't included this as part of my route. However, you can take this turn off to travel northwards and drive onto Castle Island where there are the ruins of a small tower, but my advice is to continue along the A25 and enjoy it for what it is. In the summer you will likely encounter other bikers testing their machinery on this road.

As I travel along this road my speed increases, the higher revs creating a hypnotic hum beneath me and I am in my own personal heaven. I overtake slower cars in what seems like a single sweeping motion, no thought, just instinct governing my actions. I am alone, but not lonely in any way. I have become one with the bike and the road in a seemingly single entity.

As I continue east, the southern shore of the lough comes into view, the water echoes the clear sky, only the plethora of islands and their green speckles disturb the infinity of blue.

74

The neatly cut hedgerows give an order to the impeccable road and everything seems in its right place. The countryside is open and rolling, adding to my sense of freedom.

A section of tree tunneled road on the A25 Strangford Road (Tele Atlas, 2009, © Google Maps)

Just after a break in a cluster of trees and bounded by a low grey stone wall is a left turn off for the Myra Road. The laneway narrows considerably and there is a line of short green grass in the middle of the road that can result in a sudden loss of grip, so be careful! Approximately 700 metres travelling north along this road is a pink gate and attached cottage. This is the entrance to Myra Castle grounds and gardens in which is located Walshestown Castle and church site.

Unfortunately, both of these sites are located on private ground, so access can be difficult. The site of Myra Castle includes parkland and a garden for the house (a mock castle of sorts) dating to the 19th century. It is probable that Myra represents the Irish *Maigh Rátha* 'plain of the rath' and it is likely that the castle was built on the site of this earlier rath (NIPNP, 1978, 61).

75

The name of the townland of Walshestown is recorded as *Welshe's Town* in 1612 and as *Walshe's land* in c.1657. The final element of the place-name is the genitive form of *An Breatnach*, a form of the Gaelic surname *Breat(h)nach* which means 'Welshman' and can be anglicised as *Walsh, Welsh* or *Branagh*. (http://www.placenamesni.org).

Although the towerhouse of Walshestown is probably of late 16th century date, the 1306 taxation refers to the earlier church of *Cnokengarre*. Two 13th century coffin lids were reported and recorded as originating from the associated graveyard. (SMR, 1993, DOW031:010). Interestingly Reeves records that:

> The chapel, traditionally called 'St. Mary's' stood near the Anglo-Norman castle of Walshestown. (Reeves, 1847, 40).

Given that there was a medieval chapel with medieval coffin lids it is distinctly possible that there was a Norman fort on the site of the later towerhouse as Reeves suggests.

The medieval coffin lids recovered from the chapel site associated with Walshestown Castle (JDCHS, 1939, 55)

The castle, to me, is a rather forlorn structure – dull gray but well preserved in terms of height, but my visit was exceptionally brief as it is on private land and therefore not an easily accessible tourist monument.

The surrounding countryside is awe inspiring and ideal for a painter or photographer, although I have never tried to fit an easel and paints onto the rack or in the panniers of my bike! Unfortunately I didn't get the opportunity to explore the overgrown area - probably housing the chapel remains - to the south of the castle and the location of the medieval coffin lids.

The castle and area around was used in the filming of Game of Thrones and also doubled as 'The Kingsroad' in the scene where Arya Stark releases the caged convicts – art imitating history.

Chapter Four

South Side ∫ Audleystown to Lisbane

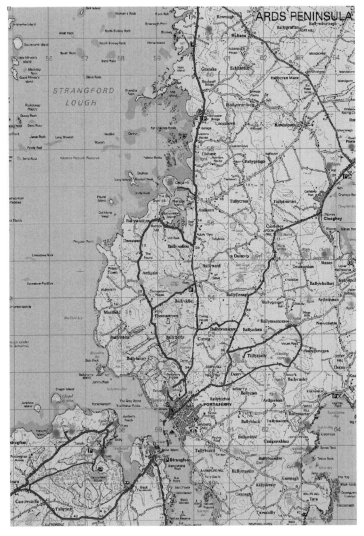

The suggested route from Walshestown across the narrows to the Ards Peninsula

78

The small area that comprises the Audleystown 'peninsula' is, perhaps, the area most densely packed with things to see and upstanding remains. Even writing about it almost leaves me out of breath and my mind darts from one site to another frenetically. I have transposed some of the known sites from the Sites and Monuments Record onto an aerial photograph using the SMR grid references for each site to attempt to plot them accurately. I have also circled a few curious features visible in the aerial image that may well add to the number of lumps, bumps, ditches, walls and other landscape indicators of archaeology.

On returning to the A25 Strangford Road from the Myra Road, only about three hundred metres travelling east, is a left turn for the Audleystown Road. I advise you take this left turn - the road will not disappoint! It is flanked on the right by a wall which I think marks the boundary of the Castle Ward estate. The road is very narrow but exceptionally rewarding, though oncoming cars can present problems. The rising crests are my personal favourite. On this section, with the bike going light as the apex is reached, I really have to use my weight to wrestle the bike and make it change direction quickly. As the greenery flashes by, the smell of the trees and pine fills my nose - I feel alive!

The road is almost magical, making you feel like you have discovered some long lost track and the engine noise echoes off the walls and trees enclosing it. The occasional breaks in the trees open the noise up in your ears with the pitch changing as a result. The Metzeler tyres kick up the loose stones as the back wheel bites onto the tarmac, a feeling of pure satisfaction!

The usual ubiquitous brown sign marks a track-way on the left, which you can follow to the Audleystown Cairn. Although the track is narrow there is parking at the bottom. Audleystown goes by a multitude of names and descriptions: horned cairn, court cairn and court tomb.

Aerial image of the Audleystown area (Annotations by Author) Aerial image from Bing Maps © Microsoft Corporation. Site locations from SMR Grid References.

The A25 Strangford Road showing the left turn for Audleystown
(Tele Atlas, 2009, © Google Maps)

The first things I notice when I park at the small parking bay are the views. Lough Chapel Island stands out with its strange looking hump, distant towers dot the landscape and, though I feel I could sit here and simply take it all in, I proceed towards the monument using the small, narrow, muddy track that has been trampled into the long pasture grass. The site is two fields away from the parking area and at the end of the first field outcrops of gnarled trees stand guard like ancient statues.

Almost tucked away in the corner surrounded by a green fence lies the dual court tomb. The site has two segmented galleries and forecourts at each end. As I stand on top of the small grassy mound, I have my iPod playing Jamie N Commons song *'Lead Me Home'*. I don't know if it's the song or the site but there is a feeling of desolation somehow. I sit down and close my eyes for a moment of quiet contemplation, Commons' husky and melancholy dulcet tones heightening my reflective thoughts.

81

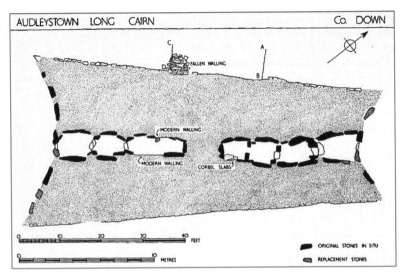

Plan of Audleystown [Long] Cairn (Collins, 1959, 22)

Audleystown – the two segmented galleries (Author)

82

The site was excavated in 1952 and forecourts containing blocking rubble lying on a roughly paved surface were recorded. Excavation also uncovered burial deposits in most, but not all, of the chambers:

> ...including burned and unburned human bones, animal bones, pottery fragments, flint implements and earth. The human remains represented about 34 individuals, male and female adults and children, one of the largest collections of human remains ever found in a prehistoric burial. (NIEA, 2009, 1).

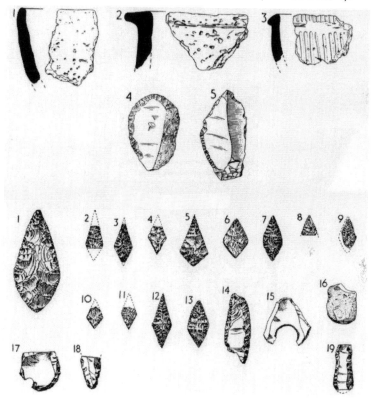

Artifacts recovered during the excavations (Collins et al, 1954 and 1959)

As the site exists today, the cairn material of local stone survives to a height of approximately two to three feet around the chambers, but this would have at one time covered the entire monument. Excavation also uncovered pottery and flint artifacts, including arrowheads and end scrapers that were undoubtedly funerary offerings.

The fact that so many individuals were buried here, whether their bodies cremated, interred or their flesh removed before burial, suggests the site at Audleystown had ritual and/or ceremonial significance. This is not surprising as the landscape here seems to exude a special feeling. Incidentally, the process of removing the flesh of an individual before burial is perhaps best illustrated by the excavation of the exhumation platform at Ballynahatty beside the Giant's Ring in Belfast. It is an impressive structure that would have had a platform for bodies to be laid out to enable the flesh to be removed, either by natural decomposition or animals.

Close up detail of one of the galleries at Audleystown (Author)

Panoramic view around Audleystown (Author)

84

To the east of Audleystown Cairn is a small roughly sub-circular enclosure that isn't apparent on initially scaning the landscape. This is Templecormick church and enclosure ruins. Quite small, they were until recently heavily overgrown and almost sucked back into the pasture farmland. A recent survey and subsequent work by Dr Philip Macdonald in 2009 added much more information and detail to previous knowledge of this site, as well as clearing much of the undergrowth and erecting a fence.

The little church was built using local stone and constructed using dry stone walling with some evidence for 'wedge' stones used instead of mortar (Macdonald, 2008, 126). The church site is surrounded by another dry stone constructed enclosure wall, which led to an early interpretation by antiquarians that it was a reused cashel. Due to the work clearing the undergrowth, Macdonald's ground plan is the first detailed one. I have also created a separate image by overlaying the Archaeological Survey of County Down's 1966 simple plan over Macdonald's for reference. Macdonald recorded thirteen grave markers within the enclosure, but records suggest burial taking place outside the walled confines as human remains were discovered during ploughing outside the enclosure wall (ASCD, 1966, 297).

The place name evidence for the site seems to be related to the nearby holy well of Tubberdoney from the Irish *Tobar Domhnaigh* or 'Sunday Well' (NIPNP, 2008, 80). There is a tantalizing potential for the place name to link back to an early Christian lineage:

> ...all churches that bear the name Domhnach were originally founded by St. Patrick, and he laid their foundations on a Sunday...having remained for seven Sundays in Cianachta, laid the foundations of seven sacred houses of the Lord, each of which he therefore called Dominica which in Irish is Domhnach. (O'Laverty, 1878, 218).

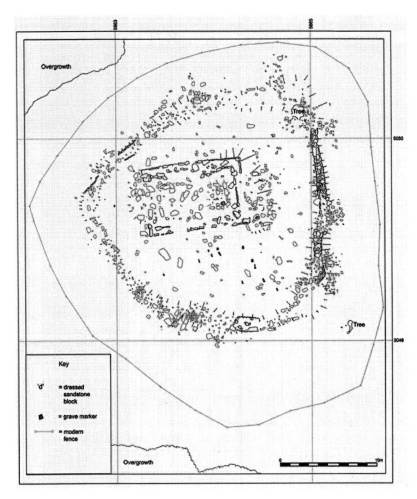

Plan of Templecormick after the recent survey (Macdonald, 2008, 127) Compare with overlay below.

When I first read this I was rather excited, but on reading Macdonald's survey account I noticed he raised a point I had completely forgotten; the presence of the nearby Chapel Island. Although there are no certainties, it is likely O'Laverty's account and place name evidence refers to that nearby site. There remains, however, so little known about the history of the idiosyncratic and enigmatic little church and enclosure, I think that very mystery of its origins and history adds to its appeal.

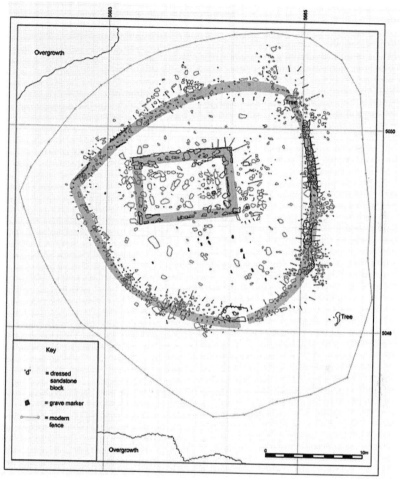

Macdonald's plan with the 1966 ASCD plan overlaid (ASCD, 1966, 297)

Further on this road is a sweeping right hand corner with the lough waters lying directly in front. However, not completely visible in the corner is a small gateway that leads down a gravel track. A car will make it down here, but on a bike the short track is glorious. In the hot summer sun the trees are blissful relief. I first rode down here on my own in the middle of

July and parked up beside a large boulder in the shade. I dismounted immediately and the stillness and quiet enabled me to shut my eyes and allow a wave of calm to wash over me. I could hear the panting of a dog and then from the trees on my left emerged a young black Labrador. He came straight over to me and was so friendly it was a moment of delight. His owners emerged from the wooded hill which leads round to the Chapel Island coastline. "He's gorgeous" I said.

"He's roasted on a day like today; we have to make sure he takes plenty of swims!"

I then noticed a faint smell of wet dog – unpleasant to some but not to me. I have always been a 'dog person' as their unconditional loyalty and strength of character make them great companions; their emotions so visible in their eyes.

The bike parked at Audley's Castle on the gravel track (Author)

To the right of this track is Audley's Castle, rising from its mound like a solemn grey pillar guarding, protecting the lough and the landscape all around. From the lough shore to the south it appears like a tower on top of a motte but the landscape is, as far as I am aware, natural. In the summer the landowner grazes cattle – including bulls – on the pasture around it. This makes for a Pamplona-esque run to the top of the mound. In autumn the sheep graze and look suspiciously at strangers entering the field, flocking together and collectively running away with the occasional alarming bleat. The views from the castle sweep over the water to Portaferry and the castle on the opposite side of the lough is visible; presumably both built to control access to the water for both trade and defense.

Audley's Castle – showing the projecting towers (Author)

What remains today is not nearly the extent of what once stood here. The towerhouse would have had an attached courtyard and buildings (a bawn). The footprint of this is still visible as a set of small walls running from the front of the castle to the steep slope to the south east. The tower has been called a "gatehouse type" because the front has a set of projecting towers like the gatehouse of an older Anglo-Norman castle type, like Carrickfergus. The entrance to the castle is between the towers which enabled a variety of defensive methods from the machicolation arch above (Dixon, 1980, 2), this would have involved all sorts of things being thrown from this arch onto would-be attackers below.

Reconstruction of Audley's Castle (Dixon, 1980, 2)

The castle is thought to date to the 15th century and built by the Audley family:

> The Audleys, of Audleystown, sold part of their property, in 1643, to the Ward family, to whom, also, they sold the remainder about the beginning of the last century; the latest mention we can find of the name in this locality being a Thomas Audley, residing in Ballynagalliagh in 1732. (H.J.W, 1853, 96).

This would tie the date of the castle with those at Sketrick and Strangford, so that period saw the erection of quite a few castles around the lough, with the likes of Quoile, Walshestown and Mahee castles slightly later. This must have represented some frenetic activity, quarrying and transporting stone, landscaping, building etc. The same author suggests in another article that the Audley family were of Anglo-Norman descent, arriving in the area with John de Courcy:

It was not until 1297, that, at a Parliament, held in Dublin, it was enacted, or rather agreed, that the first Sheriff for the liberties of Ulster should be appointed ... But it does not seem that the crown acted immediately on this order, as no Sheriff of Ulster appears until sometime afterwards, when we find the Maundevells, Audleys, Eussells, and Halywoods, all Ulster families, acting as Sheriffs. The earliest mention of the "Barons of Ulster," is in that from King John, addressed to them, 6th year of his reign, stating that if they did not cause their lord, John de Courcy, to come to the King's service, as they were bound, and gave hostages to do, he, the King would seize on their hostages and estates. (H.J.W, 1853, 41).

Whether the origins of the Audley family lie in the Anglo-Norman incursion I am, in truth, not sure. Interestingly though, and like so much round this part of County Down, the area around the castle was used as a set in Game of Thrones for Robb Stark's encampment.

I returned from visiting the castle/towerhouse to the gravel track, took off my jacket as I propped myself up against a rock and lit a cigarette - I use the jacket as a pillow of sorts. On such occasions the sun peeps through the leaves and shafts of light appear to dance on the grass and earth and everything sounds so distant. The place makes me feel like I am in a protective bubble. My calm was, however, disturbed by a car driving up the lane, stopping, then pulling over to park. A tall man in his late fifties or early sixties stepped out and gave me a friendly wave. He came over to inspect the bike, telling me that he often comes to picnic here as it's quiet as well as beautiful...he isn't wrong! I suddenly feel possessive of the area, it is my secluded spot. I see others as invading and intruding on my meditative state. But I cannot think in that absurd way for long as, with an infectious smile, he offers me - a stranger - a cup of tea. I made a mental note to come back and have done so subsequently many times, not then realising that I'd be back the next day!

I found an 'as new' Givi topbox in an online sales site and picked it up that evening. The thing was huge and would do nicely for what I had planned. My other half had gained confidence in riding pillion, even actively enjoying the experience. She had already cut her teeth on the ABR (Adventure Bike Rider) Rally in the Mourne Mountains the previous May, riding pillion on rough roads in the mountains - something that I was also new to. The plan was for both of us to visit Castle Ward on the bike and bringing a picnic with us.

We took the same glorious road down to Castle Ward arriving at the back entrance by the shore, which is marked by the small three storey towerhouse, this comprises the 'Old Castle Ward.' This area was an old farm associated with the estate. The small towerhouse has been tentatively dated to the 16th century.

On arrival we parked outside the gates on a small grass area bounded by tall trees. We could see small flies hovering over the lough surface on the warm morning sunshine; what I think were swifts or swallows darting and swooping over the water to catch them on the wing. We quickly got changed out of the stifling bike gear into shorts, t-shirts and hiking boots and sat down on a traditional blanket to eat our sandwiches. She had brought a lemon ice tea concoction. I stuck to the altogether tastier Ribena option! There are tastes from my youth that even now bring comfort and Ribena is one of those. The picnic will remain in my memory for the rest of my life, one of those perfect days that make life worth living.

After eating I parked the bike beside the little towerhouse. Due to the later insertion of a clock it has the appearance of a small old clock tower rather than a towerhouse. At the time of our visit the old buildings had been given over to local artists. There is a commune 'vibe' to the place with sculpture, crafts and paintings surrounding the building, sitting apparently easily and naturally in the post-medieval space, as if they were always supposed to be there.

92

The bike (with new topbox) parked on the Castle Ward shoreline for a picnic (Author).

The lough reflected the sunlight in the most glorious shades of blue, forming a breathtaking backdrop. The indigenous woodland follows the drumlin slopes right down to the lough shore, akin to a primeval landscape, but complementing the lough and making the waters look exceptionally inviting. I don't know if it is because it is a rare sight these days or whether it is the overall composition of the view, but at times it can look almost unreal, 'cartoonified' and like a film set backdrop rather than a view of an actual place. The ambiance encourages a stroll rather than a brisk walk, which heightens and promotes the relaxing atmosphere. The whole scene gently spreads a calm sensation over me, softly and tenderly.

Like so many sites here and in the vicinity, Castle Ward was also used in the filming of 'Game of Thrones'. The site was used as a set to film parts of Winterfell, the ancestral seat of the Starks. The grounds of Castle Ward Forest Park were

93

used for the scenes of the Lannister encampment in the first season as well as the setting for the scenes of the Riverlands.

The lough waters forming the backdrop to Old Castle Ward (Author)

As we explored the grounds, the true scale of the estate became apparent – it is huge. Again, the scenery seems a bit fake, as everything is on a monumental scale. The trees are truly massive and it seems they can't be real. The more heavily wooded areas give way to pasture land that has more sporadic tree coverage (Deer Park). The grounds and walks alone, never mind the main manor house, can take a day to explore properly. So, it's well worthwhile spending some time in the area. The formal gardens are near the main house and lie to the north and north-west. They contrast with the wild landscaping that makes up the bulk of the lands. The gardens in that way almost provide a bridge from that wildness to the formality of the manor house.

94

The current large country manor house is mid-18th century in date. It represents a phase in a long line of development, building and landscaping by various generations of the Ward family and their spouses.

> Bernard [Ward] had inherited a house ... at Castle Ward referred to "as a large and handsome Improvement of Mr Justice Ward" (Harris, Ancient and Present State of Co. Down, Dublin 1744). The architect was perhaps Richard Cassels, who died in 1750 ... Mrs Delany stayed at the earlier house in 1760 and found it "altogether one of the finest places I ever saw". ... [However, Bernard Ward] desired a larger and statelier mansion and began planning Castle Ward." (PRONI, 2007, 7).

The splitting of the facades into two completely contrasting styles (neo classical and gothic) reflects the respective tastes of Bernard Ward and Lady Anne, his wife.

> Among the current fashions in architecture was the Gothick and this was the style favoured by the whimsical Lady Anne. Her husband preferred the more conventional Classical idiom. The result was a compromise that cost £40,000 to build, and produced a house possessing the unusual feature of contemporaneous fronts in both the Classical and Gothick styles. (Ibid).

Personally I much prefer the classical façade to the gothic one. However, I know plenty of individuals who have visited the site who prefer the gothic façade. In any case, it is the latter that has the views over the lough, with open pasture and meadow sloping down to the shore. This is preferable to the parkland views that the classical side overlooks. I have been inside the house and the ground floor rooms were smaller than I had anticipated. The entrance hall, although beautiful, is somewhat underwhelming as I entered expecting some cavernous expanse.

There are a myriad of hidden paths and woodland walks, all of which are worth exploring. Wear suitable shoes though - hiking round this part of the countryside in biking leathers, boots and associated regalia would soon become tiresome!

Castle Ward House; looking at the neo-Classical façade (Author)

The easiest way to get back onto the A25, which has now become the Castleward Road, is to drive through the estate and out the main entrance gates, turning left and following the signs for Strangford. The road is smooth and an 'S' bend heaven and therefore a genuine pleasure to ride. Only about 150 to 200 metres from the estate entrance is a causeway with the waters opening up to the left hand side. Coming up on the crest of a hill, the road descends straight down towards the harbour, and the main square in the village of Strangford is exceptionally quaint. The main village is agreeably small, sitting quietly on the shore of the lough. It's hard to get lost in the village as it is so small but also well sign-posted. There are a few sites to see but the main activity here will be getting the ferry from Strangford across to Portaferry.

The namd 'Strangford', as pointed out in the first chapter, is a derivative of the Norse *Strangr-fjǫrðr* or *Strandfjörthr,* meaning 'The Strong Fjord' or 'Strong Sea-Inlet'. In Irish the village is known as *Baile Loch Cuan* or 'town on Strangford Lough' /

'town on Lough of the Harbours'. (NIPNP, 2008, 79). The harbour area is the main focus of town life and on the left hand side is a small tower behind some modern houses. The small towerhouse is a three storey building set close to the lough shore. It is thought to be a 15th century towerhouse remodeled in the 16th century and an example of a typical merchant's residence. The tower now sits as a single monument but it has been argued that there probably would have been an attached range of buildings or small bawn associated with the tower (Dixon, 1980, 5). As well as architectural features which date the earlier structure, it was also recorded as being in a state of dilapidation in 1540 (Waterman, 1967, 83). The original entrance would have been at first floor level, now blocked and replaced with a ground floor entrance.

Every time I have visited the site I get the distinct sensation that the town is a natural pit stop, sitting by the castle is a well-earned rest. On the Adventure Bike Rider rally in May 2013 - that ride led by *'Loudpedal'* - we also stopped here for what seemed like a natural break after visiting St. John's lighthouse further down the coast. As I stood in the harbour on the small pier, my eyes were drawn to a few curious features. Firstly is the towerhouse described, but there are other features: a beautifully stone lined quay with small boats sheltering from the tidal waters. The stones draw the eye as the entire quay wall is built from large stones, set vertically rather than horizontally. I remember visiting this on a post-graduate field trip and the lecturer informing us that it was a post-medieval construction.

The locally produced information leaflets by the Strangford Lough and Lecale Partnership state that:

> In 1629 Payne built the Old Quay 'where there was none before, that the biggest shippe the King hathe may lay her side beside it'. Such advantages contributed to Strangford's enhancement, and before the end of the century it had replaced Ardglass as the main port of Lecale. It is one of the best examples of a medium-sized quay in Strangford Lough that remains from the time. It is an excellent stone pier constructed

of flat stones set vertically; with an absolute minimum of mortar. (SLLP, 2012, 5).

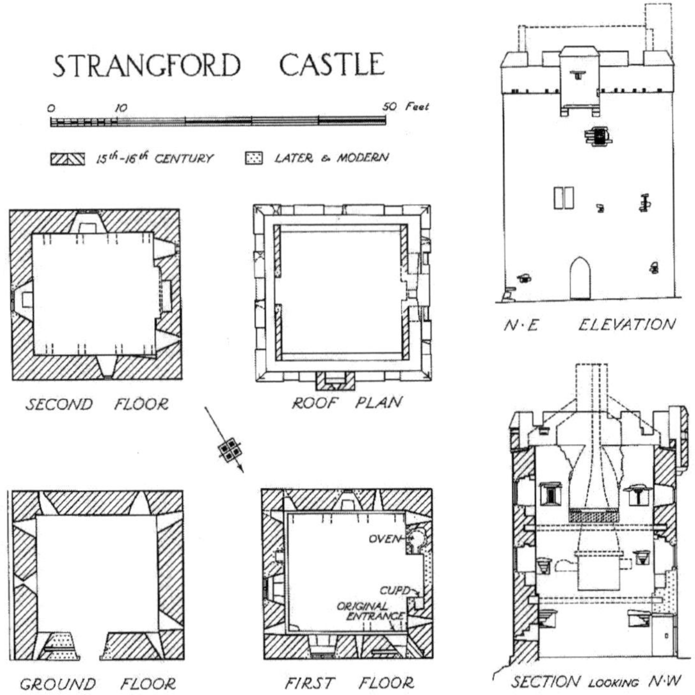
STRANGFORD CASTLE
0 10 50 Feet
15th-16th CENTURY
LATER & MODERN
SECOND FLOOR
ROOF PLAN
N·E ELEVATION
OVEN
CUPD
ORIGINAL ENTRANCE
GROUND FLOOR
FIRST FLOOR
SECTION LOOKING N·W

Plan of Strangford Castle (Waterman, 1967, 84)

Small fishing boats are drawn up on the ground surrounding the quay, adding to the quaint image the small cottages already creates.

Just beyond the quay and on private land is a curious round tower that I have only been able to view from the water's edge. The Sites and Monuments Record details a post-medieval tower (DOW032:002), describing it as three quarters round in plan and two storeys high, possibly a flanking tower at the south-east corner of a now disappeared enclosure. The grid reference in the SMR does correspond to the tower in the image. It is intriguing to think that there might have been some castle-like enclosure at this location and it is a shame that more is not known or there were not more physical remains. If

Strangford Castle looking roughly north-east (Author)

The Triumph parked at the harbour during the ABR rally (Author)

The post-medieval quay at Strangford (Author)

there had been an enclosure, it certainly would have given the harbour a more fortified and imposing appearance. The earlier Ordnance Survey maps do record towers (plural) on the site calling it 'Old Court', *An tSeanchúirt* in Irish.

There is also information on a site known as Sarah's Well which was used as a bathing pool. However, the information in the Strangford Lough and Lecale Partnership leaflet records a tower where locals would change for a swim and dry off again. Whether this activity also took place in the tower below, or whether in a separate monument I don't know, but it does seem a little unlikely, given that it is on private land and not immediately next to the water's edge.

An tSeanchúirt round tower on private land in Strangford harbour (Author)

The ferry to Portaferry from Strangford is, not even in the context of this book, a great journey to undertake. My understanding is that although the distance isn't great, the ferry powers up against the strong currents and subsequently 'drifts' down to the opposing harbour. The price for a motorbike can vary, but the only alternative is to travel all the way back in the direction just visited and to then come round the peninsula, so for both practical reasons, as well as for sheer enjoyment, the ferry is really the only viable option (the route is 0.6 nautical miles and takes approximately 8 minutes).

The boat creaks and has a certain functional charm but that's all it needs. It's similar in that way to the ferry between Ballycastle and Rathlin Island. A luxury liner it certainly isn't! But it is more romantic and the better for that. The whole craft shudders and vibrates as it makes the crossing. Nothing to worry about though. Just take in the views!

Although there are medieval remains in Portaferry, as best I can research, the town, appears to have developed in the post-medieval era, mainly during the 16th and 17th centuries. The old church site is referred to as *Ecclesia de Felipton* but the name Portaferry is comparatively modern and not the name of a parish (Chart *et al*, 1940, 109).

On arriving in Portaferry, the ferry docks at The Strand that runs parallel with the bay. You will see the parapet of Portaferry Castle just above the houses. Here you can take the first turn right then immediately left at the Portaferry Hotel and onto Castle Street. At the top of this short street, on your left, lie the ruins of Portaferry Castle. The monument seems to sit easily in the town with no feeling of incongruity about its place in the landscape - unlike some other sites visited. The castle overlooks the narrow straits in partnership with Strangford Castle. The castle is reputed to have formed the heart of the extensive estates of the Savage family (Dixon, 1980, 3). The Savages' lands were:

> ...principally in the Ardes, where they resided in their Castles of Portaferry, Ardkeen, and Ballygalgot; yet they were occasionally designated 'Lords of Leathcathail' [Lecale,] but this was only at short intervals, when with the strong-hand they over-ran the territory, until driven back to their peninsular highlands by the yet stronger forces of the O'Neills, and finally by the Fitzgeralds. (H.J.W, 1853, 95).

There is some debate over the exact date of the origin of the towerhouse. One suggestion is that it was built in the early 16th century and there are records to show it was repaired in 1635 with the work including:

> ...roofing and flooring it, and by striking out longer lights, with free-stone window-cases: and also building (and joining to it) a fair slated stone house, as may be seen, with the Savage's and Montgomery's arms above the door thereof. (ASCD, 1966, 245).

The 1940 Preliminary Survey of Ancient Monuments of Northern Ireland, however, states:

The oldest portion of the castle may probably be dated as of the 15th century. So far as one can judge from Savage Armstrong's books, it was at this period the Savages of Portaferry branched off from the parent stock of Ardkeen. (Chart, *et al*, 1940, 109).

It would make sense for the castle to be contemporary with those at Strangford and Audley's – though I think that this may be a gut reaction, rather than one based on any evidence. Press me for an answer and I am unable to give one! Lawlor, writing in the latter account, does advise caution. He was apparently unable to get to the interior to date the castle from the finer architectural detailing. There is a slight suggestion of an attached wall that may have formed part of the later attached house, although this structure has gone. Recent archaeological monitoring recorded that the site had been substantially disturbed and nothing of archaeological significance was recorded (SMR DOW 032:003). Now, though, the castle is somewhat forlorn, with walls crumbling and shrubbery protruding from the centre of the tower. It appears that the town owes its origin to the castle and its strategic site, rather than developing on some ancient pre-existing settlement. Lewis records in his Topographical Dictionary of Ireland that the castle was:

...built by the first of the Savage family who came into this part of the country with John de Courcy, shortly after the arrival of the English, and the place being well secured and garrisoned by that powerful family, its situation on the strait made it a post of great importance in all the subsequent wars, during which neither it nor the neighbouring district of the Southern Ardes ever fell into the hands of the Irish; but the town, until lately, was only a small collection of cottages built under the shelter of the castle. (Lewis, 1837, 1144).

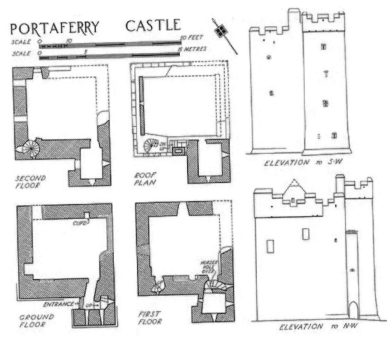

Elevation and Plan of Portaferry Castle (ASCD, 1966, 246)

Portaferry Castle (Author)

If there was something there at the time of de Courcy's incursion into Ireland, as Lewis suggests, then it also implies there was a pre-existing fortification before the more modern tower. Perhaps this is why the monument appears to sit so easily in the modern town; the entire place grew up with it and alongside it. The castle site is somewhat boxed in by the modern street layout. If you turn immediately right beside the castle and then left onto the Square leading to Church Street, you will find Templecran[n]ey Church site, also known as Ballyphilip. It is situated on the left hand side in a wooded thicket. Set among the trees, the clearing feels secluded and 'holy'. It is strange how some sites, like Nendrum and Inch Abbey, exude this spiritual quality. Here is no different, though it is on a much smaller scale. The history of the site predates the current upstanding ruins, which are variously dated to be from the 17th or 18th centuries. However, the site exists within an older burial ground, and it is thought that there was an earlier church here called *Ecclesia de Feliipton* from the 1306 taxation roll (ASCD, 1966, 309).

The site, then, has two name variations; that of its earlier *Felipton* to Ballyphilip and Templecran[n]ey.

> Ballyphilip is first attested in English, as a parish name: Ecclesia de Felipton, in the papal taxation c. 1306. The personal name Philip was popular among the Anglo-Norman settler but the individual is unidentified. The church remained that of Phillipstowne in early 17th century church records. After 1657 the majority of references are to Ballyphilip, Baile Philib (Muhr, 2004).

It was Reeves who 'located' Templecranney in Ardquin parish.

Reeves assumes that it was built because the original church was outside the town. The first element is clearly teampall [church], not used before the second millennium. The most likely second element in a church name is a saint's name, but the most similar personal name here is a Crónán who was abbot of Bangor d.668. Teampall Crannaí [church of the stake-fence] from Crannach meaning wooden, or something made of wood. The pronunciation of the second element as 'krah-ni' and is difficult to interpret. (*Ibid*).

The site is seen as unique as it has been suggested that an annex on the north side would have been a priest's 'kitchen' or living apartment (Chart *et al*, 1940, 109).

Templecraney Church ruins (Author)

106

Templecraney Church ruins – with tower (Author)

When I visited the site it was a hot day with the skies clear, apart from several wispy clouds. Even with as much of my kit off as possible – back armour, armoured jacket, armoured gloves and helmet – I felt parched and overheated; my dry sandpaper-like tongue sticking to the roof of my mouth. The heat made my eyes heavy and after draining a bottle of water at an alarming rate. I lay down under the trees, the shade provided a haven from the heat. I let the hustle and gentle 'hum' of the town fade into the background as I dozed off in a completely calm, almost Zen-like state.

On leaving Templecraney, you can follow the road straight to the bottom of Church Street. It will narrow and the houses, small and tightly packed, give one a sensation of being hemmed in. The sound of the bike's exhaust (I have an aftermarket Blueflame Performance on mine) reverberates off the enclosed spaces. Although I find it joyous, I'm sure the residents aren't quite so enamored! At the bottom of Church Street is a dimple roundabout. Here you turn right, following the directional signage for the A2 to Cloughey / Cloghy and Donaghadee. Due to the town's one way system, this will filter onto Ann Street, then left onto High Street (all the while following the signs for Cloughey / Cloghy), High Street morphs into the A2. The road widens slightly and becomes less urban, leaving the houses and schools behind, it begins to ribbon through the countryside. The gradual left and right bends punctuate the short straights until a sharp almost 90° right-hand bend, beyond which is the national speed limit sign.

This is a road I really enjoy. It seems to me very 'giving' when you are on a bike, but be wary of the occasional horse rider that can suddenly appear around a corner. Once you are past another switchback left hand corner, the open manicured fields on the left contrast with the unkempt trees and gorse on the right - as if the road acts as some sort of border keeping the wildness at bay. Approximately 450 metres beyond this, on the right is an off-shoot laneway, filtering off from the road and leading up to houses perched above the A2. I have pulled in here, as parking on the main road is impossible. The additional 120 metres on the A2 to the site entrance has to be on foot. The site is marked by a green arrow sign on the right of the road for Derry Churches – although this may seem like a bit of a faff, I think the site is well worth it.

The narrow grass pathway meanders up to the dual church site. The name is derived from *Dere* meaning 'an oak wood' (Reeves, 1847, 23). The churches apparently celebrate the festival of St. Cumain in May of each year (*Ibid*, 24). The text from the *Felire of Aengus*, a text written probably *c.*800AD on the festology of the saint, suggests that there were;

> ... three virgins named Cumain, daughter of Allen, or three churches dedicated under the invocation of a holy virgin of that name, one of which was that of Derry in the Ards. (O'Laverty, 1878, 405).

Interestingly, excavation in 1962 found burials underneath and earlier than the existing buildings. There was also evidence that the currently visible buildings overlay earlier structures of a different orientation with occupation debris also found under the north church, though it was not proved to be ecclesiastical in nature (Hamlin, 2008, 612 - 613). A cist is a stone-lined grave, the stone lining forms a 'coffin' of sorts; all the burials beneath the south church were in cists, with cist burials also located between the buildings. If these cist burials were the earlier method of burial, the plain burials beneath the north church were later and represent an extension to the original burial ground (Waterman, 1967, 56). The current south church is smaller and thought to be earlier than the north church building. It is also in the north church that a small early cross-carved stone is located.

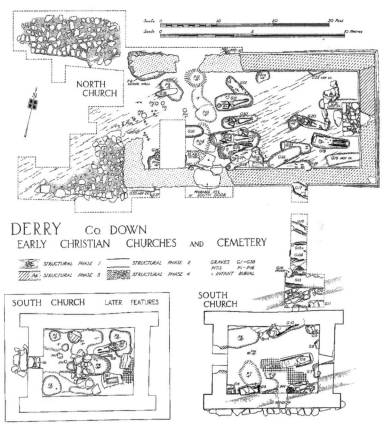

Plan of the excavation findings (Waterman, 1962, 54 - 55)

109

The interiors of both buildings were used, after their abandonment, for the burial of infants. Such a place is referred to as a *cillín* (*Ibid*, 63). This is a rather tragic facet of history. It represents, almost in a tangible act, the parents' desperate desire to have their children buried in consecrated ground, but as the infants had not been baptized at the time of their death, they were not eligible to be interred in functioning church cemeteries. The practice was not uncommon throughout Ireland. I worked on an excavation at Castle Carra in Antrim where the site had also been used for this practice. The scene it conjures is exceptionally sad.

The dating the churches is difficult. Their construction has been hypothesized as somewhere between the 10th and 12th centuries. However, although Waterman is cautious, he suggests a construction date for the current remains as the early 12th century (1100's) with later extensions to the buildings in the 13th century. The site sits on top of earlier 'Early Christian' deposits and these are, presumably, 7th – 9th century. His excavation also found a buckle that he dated to the 7th – 8th centuries (*Ibid*, 68 – 69). He suggests that the site was founded as a small monastery or more likely some form of communal hermitage.

The churches are a little odd as they seem perched in the landscape in isolation – although this was probably the intention. The consequence is they don't seem to relate to any aspect of the environment now. Whether the marshy ground surrounding them was at one time flooded I am unsure, if this were the case then they would have been on something of an island and in that context make more sense. I felt quite exposed and lonely on the site, and the buildings seemed more eerie than spiritual, although I am sure this is because I was aware of their use as a *cillín*. A shudder of vulnerability comes over me and I am uncomfortable.

·EMJ·1951·

Reconstruction of the Derry Churches (Jope, 1952)

There are two route options available to cut across from the A2 Cloughey Road to the A20 Rowreagh Road: the first is a by-way open to traffic which is the first left immediately after leaving the site. This is a track with grass in the middle, but if off-roading, of sorts, is the desired pastime then this is definitely the route to take. Initially stony and technically challenging, it gradually becomes concreted towards the end at the junction with the A20. Alternatively, you may continue on the A2, where approximately, 1.5 kilometres past the site, just after a hard left hand bend delineated by squat stone walls on either side, there is a veering to the left called the Loughdoo Road. It is also marked by directional signs for Donagadee, which is straight ahead, and Portaferry, which is behind on the A2 itself. You may take this road for several kilometres until the lough waters come into view again, then turn right following the signs for Kircubbin and Newtownards.

111

Chapter Five

The Last Leg ∫ Homeward Bound

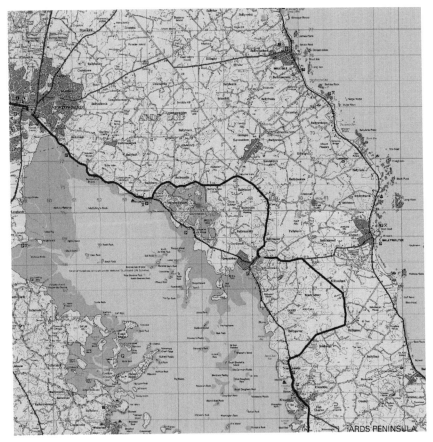

Suggested route from Kircubbin to Newtownards

The A20 (Rowreagh Road) is one I adore; the surface is good and there are combinations of long undulating straights as well as undulating cambered and off-camber corners, all of which are spectacularly situated beside the lough's eastern shore. Being perched higher up on a bike than in a car enables one to peer over the hedgerows to fully appreciate the views, and the hedgerows add to the sense of speed. Whether by fate or by design, I have tended to travel this road in glorious weather and, as a result, my memories of it are with the lough shimmering in a light turquoise blue in my peripheral vision with the pleasant smell of a warm salt water shore hovering in the air. The road can be busy, but the ample straights mean overtaking the slower traffic is not a problem. This is part of the journey where simply being on the bike is the only experience I need. All other thoughts are cleared from my head and the act of biking on this road becomes the only facet to my conscious self.

One should go past the Rubane Road on the right. This leads to Portavogie and Kirkistown. Kirkistown, by the way, has a castle as well as a racetrack!). The small town now directly ahead is Kircubbin. The origins of the town's name are somewhat unclear with two schools of thought: the first is that it comes from the Irish *Cill Ghobáin* probably meaning St. Gobán's church. St. Ghobáin/ Gobán was a Benedictine monk who died in 670. Interestingly, it is not uncommon for similar place names, especially in Scotland, to have the '*cill*' replaced with '*kirk*' with this being a Scottish derivative which means 'residence near a church' e.g., Kirkcolm. This substitution appears to have been the origin for the suffix in the first part of Kircubbin. The second school of thought suggests that the name's origins are derived from a written grant by William de Maudeville. Kircubbin is referred to as *Cubynhillis in Tenemento de Ynchemkargy* or *Cubyn a temement of Inishargy*. This is also suggested in the 1306 Papal Taxation which refers to:

Ecclesia de Sacti Medumy - beside the church of "Inyscargi" (Inishargy) - translated this means "The church of Saint Medumy." (Galloway, 2000, 1).

The ecclesiastical site identified as Inishargy lies several kilometres to the north east of the town, (recorded in the Sites and Monuments Record as DOW 018:001 and can be seen at Irish Grid Reference J60400 64740). The term *Inyscargi* roughly translates as 'island of the rock' and the town's origins can be linked to St. Modomnocus also known as *Modomnoc of Ossory* who died c.550 AD (Reeves, 1847, 19).

The town itself is not one I am overly fond of. It is usually quite busy and I tend to simply drive through it. However, just outside and to the north of the village is a natural quay and harbour with a parking area. You can pull over at this point and catch your breath while looking out over the lough. There is a small information board outlining the different types of wildlife, particularly birds, within the maritime landscape. Continuing on the A20 further outside the village, the road has a long sweep to the right. Once through this, there is a right turning marked conveniently by a church and the road is also marked for Ballywalter. You can take this turning onto the Inishargy Road.

The Inishargy Road immediately narrows in the more rural 'B' road, and is, initially at least, long and straight, which gives the brain time to relax slightly. The fields with their patchy tufts of longer marshy grass billow in the wind. The scene is only periodically punctuated by small residential dwellings. On a straight section just over five kilometres on this road is a left turning that cuts between two such fields. It has no signposts and initially appears to be a track or private road. It isn't. This is the Killyvolgan Road. The white lines stop approximately twenty metres after you turn off, the road surface is rougher than the smoother tarmac that preceded it but it is, in my experience, rare to find another vehicle on it. As a result I have the feeling that I own the road. This is the 'back way' to Greyabbey. For the more direct route simply carry on the A20, hugging the coast outside Kircubbin. Approximately 800 metres on the Killyvolgan Road is a left turn onto the Blackabbey Road. The hedgerows immediately become taller and less manicured making me feel that I am in a green tunnel which is an experience I enjoy. It seems to help me focus on what's ahead. The road straightens, noticeably overhung by trees in places and, where there are some, the houses are set back off the road at some distance, adding to the sensation of isolation, which is a comfort. The road is drag-strip straight until you come to a 'Give Way' sign, turn left here onto the Ballywalter Road.

The Ballywalter Road runs behind the beautiful mid-18th century Rosemount Estate and Grey Abbey House. Just after a downhill, right hand bend, there is an imposing wall on the left – this wall is the rear boundary of the estate grounds. This road morphs into the B5 Church Street, without a sign or notice. But the name change is significant as it now enters Greyabbey. Keeping the wall on the left, there is an opening in the trees with the ruins of the abbey clearly visible – this is our next destination. You turn left into the gardened visitor centre to park at the Abbey. From the centre, it is a short walk through the trees to the clearing on which the site is situated.

Every time I have been here I have been the only one there, at least for a time. This has always surprised me. The site is nestled in the trees and is, for that reason alone, never mind the spectacular ruins, almost magical. I find myself at peace once more and, as always at this sort of site, some form of spiritual calm descends on me.

Greyabbey is in the finest tradition of a ruined Irish monastic site. The name is derived from the Irish *Mainistir Laith* 'abbey/monastery grey'. The site was founded by Affreca (*Athbhreac*), wife of John de Courcy and daughter of Godfred, King of Man, in 1193.

Its Latin name was de Iugo Dei 'of the yoke of God', but at that date it was also called Whit[e] Abbey and in 1491 Grey Abbey in English. In 1585 it was referred to as Hore Abbey (al Leighe al Iugo Dei), where Leighe seems to represent Irish liath 'grey' as the equivalent of English hoar 'frosty white'. The anglicised

115

spelling Monesterlee in 1603 represents the Irish version Mainistir Liath (Muhr, 2004).

I think settlements that grew up around an earlier structure or focal point in antiquity have a different feel to more modern 'planned' urban centres. The pace of life seems slower and nothing seems to matter as much. The parodied Irish thought process of *"Ach sure, it'll be grand"*, seems to fit more comfortably somehow.

The first building encountered is the main church; interestingly this was re-roofed and altered for parochial purposes until 1778. The church is entered on the west side by a magnificent pointed, early Gothic door with Romanesque carving and decoration. The stonework and decoration has been referred to as an early example of the Irish Transitional building of directly English origin (ASCD, 1966, 275). Furthermore, the type and decoration of the door means that it was probably not completed before *c.*1220 (*Ibid*), with the bulk of the abbey buildings constructed of the Early English period, therefore dating to 1200 – 1250 (Chart *et al*, 1940, 90). The transitional building period is so called as it aligns to a time when Ireland was both politically and architecturally in a state of flux and change, coinciding with the lands of the island being handed by Papal Bull to Henry II.

> There was an accompanying but much more rapid architectural transition from the then waning Hiberno-Romanesque to that 'first pointed' or Early English style. It was a style of architecture which supplanted, almost to annihilation, the ancient Celtic characteristics. (Phillips, 1874, 5).

The legend of the founding of the abbey states that the de Courcy's wife Affreca vowed that if she arrived safely to Ireland she would found a religious house (Hamlin, 1979, 2). The abbey was Cistercian and under 'rule' of its mother house at *Holm Cultram* in Cumberland (*Ibid*).

116

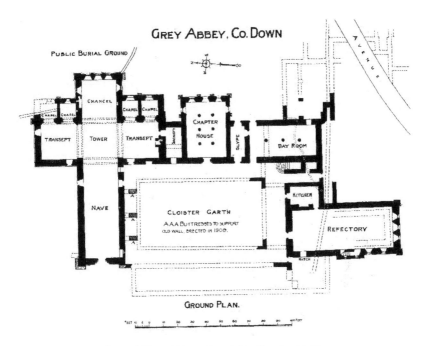

GROUND PLAN.

Ground Plan of Greyabbey (after Hamlin, 1979)

The plan of the ruins conforms to Cistercian norms, with the church at the north end of a group of buildings containing a nave, chancel and two transepts, each with two side chapels. The whole area of Greyabbey's foreshore is also of interest and importance to archaeology, containing monuments and sites from Mesolithic forests to medieval stone and wooden fish traps (Forsythe *et al*, 2007, 8). In 2000 a logboat was discovered on the foreshore of Greyabbey Bay, made of oak - the radiocarbon dating put its construction from 3499 – 3032 BC in the Neolithic period (*Ibid*).

Greyabbey is something of a contradiction for me. If approached via the Portaferry Road there are quaint buildings set on the lough shore side of the village, clad in ivy with Georgian styled front doors and sash windows, small boutique antique shops and narrow streets, presumably conforming to some medieval footprint. A small squat church sits on a street corner with a red telephone box next to its boundary. This is

117

The west entrance door (Author)

The nave and crossing looking towards the alter east end windows (Author)

118

juxtaposed against ex-council housing at the other end of Main Street. I can't help but ask what the planners were thinking in the 60's or 70's when they were erected. Despite this though, it retains its charming feel – perhaps due to much of the surrounding tree covering on the drumlins, that makes the village seem like a hidden jewel.

The ruins at the abbey encouraged me to clamber over them, uninterrupted and with no intrusion, as I ran my hands over the mouldings and stonework, trying to imagine the medieval monks' life; even attempting to romanticise it. It must have been hard. The idyllic surroundings belie the importance that the site would have had to medieval life. Whilst I contemplated this, the winds rustled the trees that surround the abbey. A familiar sensation washed over me, I was alone but in no way lonely, it is almost a state of bliss. I have, on each visit, sat down under a tree and simply contemplated life. The ruins lend themselves to it somehow as do the monastic remains at Nendrum and Inch. It is at such times that I am content - at least for the time being, until my mind starts to question everything.

It is at this moment I find myself contemplating the big questions in life; is there a God? If so, am I in his or her grace? I have become attracted to Buddhist teachings, as I find their emphasis on gentleness and kindness appealing - although I cannot call myself a Buddhist, however much I'd like to. I like the idea of reincarnation based on your deeds and behaviour, but at the same time can't quite get my head around it. I was brought up in an Anglican Christian background, although currently I think a line from the 'Usual Suspects', "to pinch and slightly alter it", sums up my beliefs. I'm not sure if there is a God, but I'm scared of him all the same. I find myself confronting my own mortality. I am at an age where the care-free attitudes I had in my youth have mutated into a more fearful realisation of death, which seems to approach faster with each increasingly quickly passing year. The irony of having this head-fuck debate in the tranquil grounds of a monastic site isn't lost on me!

What is there after death? Again, I ask questions with none of the answers. I think, probably obviously, there are two possibilities, namely there is either a complete state of nothingness or there is a conscious afterlife. The former is a state in which there is no awareness or consciousness and therefore nothing to fear. The latter is another adventure. Either way they aren't to be feared. I am, though, petrified of dying if not death itself. I wish that I held a steadfast belief that was a source of comfort and solace, rather than this bastardised form of agnosticism. In a material world, the bike is my serenity *and* my sanity.

Alas, though, from Greyabbey it's a straight slingshot homeward.

Chapter Six

Beginning of the End ∫ Reality Bites

Scrabo Tower (Author)

Scrabo Tower looms over the northern end of the peninsula, acting as a beacon for the beginning of the end. The trip is nearly over and the more rural ideal, at least as an ideological ideal, will soon be substituted for the bustle of Newtownards' urban sprawl, together with the white van and all-week 'Sunday' drivers on the Portaferry Road. The tower is a metaphor for reality; a return to the grind with the bubble well and truly burst. As a beacon for the end of the journey and my return to normality, I despise it.

"Turn back......turn back!" the message repeats over and over in my head. I can't though, and this is perhaps why I haven't done an around the world trip. Some people seem to be able to ditch their life here, leave the head pounding pressures behind - although how they pay their mortgages and bills whilst on the road I'll never know. But perhaps that last statement is why I haven't done it, I am in essence a product of western dogma – go to university, get a job, get a mortgage, get a house – the angst-ridden side of me recognises my life is full of shit I don't need. The consumer culture has me on its list of victims and, moreover, and more distressingly, I willingly succumbed and let it happen. I wish I had the vision of these travellers or (at least) their balls to do it. But why do I yearn to turn back? It's an awkward question and I can only assume that I want to escape.

The other simple reality is that most people simply cannot, for various reasons, take off around the world. As many bikers have pointed out to me whilst writing this book, there are ample opportunities for exploring our own shores and these are all too quickly discarded for caged dreams of the greener grass of far distant lands.

The bike has become, slowly, gently and quietly, my reality and it's a reality I want and one I am comfortable with. She is an old friend, a reliable companion and my trust in her is complete, representing a thorough surrender. The romanticism of riding off into the sunset remains a strong one for many of us, and I am no different, but I doubt the trip I have in my head - incident-free, carefree, seemingly endlessly funded - is in any way realistic.

Strange how stories enter your head at these sorts of junctures. I can remember watching a documentary by Michael McGarrigle – a guy who was made redundant by Shorts Bombardier in 2003 – instead of moping and thinking his world had collapsed, as many of us – myself included – would, he explored the world for three years making a BBC documentary in the process, he said:

> I don't think the word 'redundancy' was out of my manager's mouth before the door was swinging. There is a big planet out there and I'm not getting any younger. I gave up a three bedroom house, my car, my garden. Now my whole life fits into two backpacks.

I admire him immensely, and those like him.

I tend to examine myself, my soul if you will, whilst on a bike. As well as seeing sites of interest and enjoying the act of riding a motorcycle, of itself, the time on the bike is one of inward reflection. If I am honest, there are times when I do not like this process, as it forces me to confront uncomfortable truths about my past actions, thoughts and words. It can be painful, distressing even but cathartic and necessary, as my focus on these mistakes means I will not repeat them. This seems to be something of a preoccupation of mine, indeed I have tattooed on my chest: *'Quae Mihi Facienda Fuerant Omisi et Quae Facienda non Fuerant Admisi. Ignosce Mihi'* which translates as *'for what I should have done and didn't and for what I did and shouldn't, forgive me'*. It acts as a constant reminder.

I would be remiss if I didn't thank several key individuals; firstly my long suffering other half and soul mate Nicola, for allowing me the freedom to get out on these runs and trips and indulge my obsession, whilst I skimp on helping around the house! I think she knows I would be truly lost without this freedom. The older I get, the more the bike becomes an extension of me and part of who I am. She has become a pillion on several trips and I hope this continues. Secondly, Kivi for being my best friend and also for getting me into bikes in the first place – on the back of his Kawasaki Z650 in Donegal. His maroon BMW R80RT sparked the flame when we were in Portstewart. He encouraged me throughout my test and also gave me, gratis, my first bike! We still head away on the bikes and I hope to continue well into our respective dotages! Finally, my Dad for being, well, my Dad; a hero of mine in life and an example of how to live it. They have all enabled me to put - in my head at least - the world to rights by riding a motorbike.

Bibliography

Archaeological Survey of County Down (ASCD)., 1966: *An Archaeological Survey of County Down.* Belfast: Her Majesty's Stationary Office.

Balé, M. A., and Purcell, E., 2003: *The Annals of Ulster.* CELT: Corpus of Electronic Texts. *http://www.ucc.ie/celt.* University College Cork.

Bambury, P., and Beechinor, S., 2000: *The Annals of Ulster.* CELT: Corpus of Electronic Texts. *http://www.ucc.ie/celt.* University College Cork.

Brett, C. E. B., 1973: Historic Buildings, Groups of Buildings and Areas of Architectural Importance in the Towns Villages of East Down. *Ulster Architectural Heritage Society.* Belfast.

Carruthers, J., 1853: Hoards of Coins Found in Ireland. *Ulster Journal of Archaeology First Series.* Volume 1, *pp 164 – 167.* Belfast.

Chart, D. A., Evans, E. E., and Lawlor, H. C., 1940: *A Preliminary Survey of the Ancient Monuments of Northern Ireland.* Her Majesty's Stationary Office. Belfast.

Collins, A. E. P. and Proudfoot, B., 1959: A Trial Excavation at Clea Lakes Crannog, Co. Down. *Ulster Journal of Archaeology.* Volume 22, *pp 92 – 101.* Belfast.

Collins, A. E. P., 1959: Further Work at Audleystown Long Cairn, Co. Down. *Ulster Journal of Archaeology, Third Series.* Volume 22 *pp 21 – 27.* Belfast.

Darvill, T., 2008: *The Concise Oxford Dictionary of Archaeology.* Oxford University Press. Oxford.

Davies, O., 1976: Ring-Forts and Mottes. *Ulster Journal of Archaeology Third Series.* Volume 39, *pp 72 – 73.* Belfast.

Davies, R., 2001: Co. Down Northern Ireland Family History Research Site. http://freepages.genealogy.rootsweb.ancestry.com/~rosdavies/PHO TOSwords/SaulAll.htm

Dixon, H., 1980: *The Three Tower Houses, County Down*. Historic Monuments and Buildings Branch, Department of the Environment. Her Majesty's Stationary Office. Belfast.

Dunlop, W. M., 2009: Ulster Archaeological Society Newsletter. UAS. Belfast.

Edwards, N., 1996: The Archaeology of Early Medieval Ireland. Routledge. Oxon.

Evans, E. E. and Davies, O., 1934: Excavations of a Chambered Horned Cairn at Ballyalton, Co. Down. *Proceedings of the Belfast Natural History and Philosophical Society 1933 – 1934, pp 79 – 104*. Belfast

Forsythe, W., McConkey, R., and McErlean, T. C., 2002: Strangford Lough, Maritime Archaeology on the County Down Coast. *Archaeology Ireland: Heritage Guide No. 20.*

Forsythe, W., and Gregory, N., 2007: A Neolithic Logboat from Greyabbey Bay, County Down. *Ulster Journal of Archaeology Third Series,* Volume 66, *pp 6 – 13.* Belfast

Fredengren, C., 2002: Crannogs: a study of people's interaction with lakes, with particular reference to Lough Gara in the north-west of Ireland. Wordwell.

Galloway, J., 2000: Kircubbin A Short History. *Ards Borough Council.*

http://www.ards-council.gov.uk/getattachment/0cc4b4e2-af4f-4f58-a45f-78d056cade42/Kircubbin-A-Short-History-pdf.aspx

Getty, E., 1856: The Round Towers of Ulster. *Ulster Journal of Archaeology First Series.* Volume 4, *pp 128-139.* Belfast.

Hamlin, A., 1979: *Grey Abbey County Down.* Her Majesty's Stationary Office. Belfast.

Hamlin, A., and *Kerr, T (ed.).,* 2008: The Archaeology of Christianity in the North of Ireland. *British Archaeological Reports, British Series, 460.* Oxford.

H, J. W., 1853: The Anglo Norman Families of Lecale: In the County of Down. *Ulster Journal of Archaeology First Series,* Volume One, *pp 92 – 100.* Belfast.

126

H, J. W., 1853: The Earldom and Barons of Ulster. *Ulster Journal of Archaeology First Series,* Volume One, *pp 38 – 42.* Belfast.

Hondelink, F., 2002: *Annals of the Four Masters.* CELT: Corpus of Electronic Texts. *http://www.ucc.ie/celt.* University College Cork.

JDCHS, 1939: St. Mary's Knocknagar. *Down and Connor Historical Society's Journal.* Volume Ten, *pp. 55.*

Jope, E. M., 1952: *Ancient Monuments in Northern Ireland not in State Charge.* Her Majesty's Stationary Office. Belfast.

Lawlor, H.C., 1919 – 1920: Report on excavations at the mound and on the site of Rathkeltchar, Downpatrick. *Report and proceedings of the Belfast Natural History and Philosophical Society, Session 1919-20, No. 4, pp 105-120.* Belfast.

Lewis, S., 1837: A Topographical Dictionary of Ireland: Several Counties, Cities, Boroughs, Corporate, Market and Post Towns, Parishes and Villages with Historical and Statistical Descriptions. London.

MacAdam, R., 1857: Brazen Cauldrons. *Ulster Journal of Archaeology First Series,* Volume 5, *pp 82 – 90.* Belfast.

Macdonald, P., 2002: Excavations at Mahee Castle, Mahee Island, County Down. *Data Structure Report No. 11.* Centre for Archaeological Fieldwork, Queen's University. Belfast.

Macdonald, P., 2003: Nendrum, Mahee Island, County Down. *Data Structure Report No. 16.* Centre for Archaeological Fieldwork, Queen's University. Belfast.

Macdonald, P., 2008: A New Survey of Templecormick, Audleystown, County Down. *Ulster Journal of Archaeology Third Series,* Volume 67, *pp 126 – 135.* Belfast.

Mac Niociall, G., 2010: *The Annals of Tigernach.* CELT: Corpus of Electronic Texts. *http://www.ucc.ie/celt.* University College Cork.

McCormick, F., 2009: Struell Wells: Pagan past and Christian present. *Journal of the Royal Society of Antiquaries of Ireland,* Volume 139, *pp 45-62.*

McErlean, T. C., Earwood, C., Moore, D., and Murphy, E., 2007: The Sequence of Early Christian Period Horizontal Tide Mills at Nendrum Monastery: An Interim Statement. *Historical Archaeology Volume 41,*

No. 3, Maritime Archaeology in Ireland (2007), pp 63 – 75. Society for Historical Archaeology.

McKeown, R., 1934: Kilmeleyt and Kilseaclon. *Down and Connor Historical Society*, Volume 6 *pp 56 – 58.* Down.

McNeill, T. E., 1975: Ulster Mottes: A Checklist. *Ulster Journal of Archaeology Third Series.* Volume 38, *pp 49 – 56.* Belfast.

McNeill, T. E., 1980: Anglo-Norman Ulster: History and Archaeology of an Irish Barony, 1177 – 1400. John Donald Publishers Ltd. Edinburgh

Muhr, K., 2004: Northern Ireland Place Name Project. *Irish and Celtic Studies (School of Languages).* Queen's University. Belfast. http://www.ulsterplacenames.org/

Muhr, K., 2008: Place Name Information: Corporation of Killyleagh. *Northern Ireland Place-Name Project.* Belfast.

Mussen, S., 2013: Inishargy House, Kircubbin County Down. Excavation and Monitoring. *Data Structure Report No. 94.* Centre for Archaeological Fieldwork, Queen's University. Belfast.

Nevin, N., 2009: Comber Abbey and Parish - A Short History. *clydesburn.blogspot.co.uk*

Northern Ireland Environment Agency (NIEA)., 1993: Sites and Monuments Record (SMR). http://www.doeni.gov.uk/niea/built-home.htm

Northern Ireland Environment Agency (NIEA)., 2005: Nendrum, County Down. *Environment and Heritage Service Site Guide.* Belfast.

Northern Ireland Environment Agency (NIEA)., 2009: County Down Prehistoric Monuments. *Northern Ireland Environment Agency.* Belfast. http://www.doeni.gov.uk/niea/07_ph_monuments_co_down.pdf

NIPNP., 1987 – 2007: Northern Ireland Place Name Project. Queen's University. Belfast. http://www.ulsterplacenames.org/PDF%20Files/Postal%20Towns%20-%20Bailte%20Poist.pdf

Ó Baoill, R., 2011: Archaeological excavations at Quoile Castle, Co. Down. *Data Structure Report No. 85.* Centre for Archaeological Fieldwork, Queen's University. Belfast

O'Donovan, J., 2009: Annala Rioghachta Eireann: Annals of the Kingdom of Ireland by The Four Masters, From The Earliest Period To The Year 1616. BiblioBazaar.

O'Laverty, J., 1878: An Historical Account of the Diocese of Down and Connor Volume One. J. Duffy. Dublin.

O'Rahilly, C., 1976: Táin Bó Cuailgne, Recension I. CELT: Corpus of Electronic Texts. Dublin.

Patterson, W. H., 1892: On Some Ancient Sculptured Slabs at Saul, County Down. *The Journal of the Royal Society of Antiquaries of Ireland Fifth Series.* Volume 2, *pp 432 – 433.*

Phillips, J. J., 1874: St. Mary's of Grey Abbey, County Down, Ireland, as Existing in the Year A.D 1874. *Records of the Medieval Architecture of Ireland and Belfast Architectural Association.* Belfast.

Public Record Office of Northern Ireland (PRONI)., 2007: Introduction Ward Papers. Crown Copyright. Belfast.

Reeves, W., 1847: Ecclesiastical Antiquities of Down, Connor, and Dromore. Hodges and Smith. Dublin.

SLLP., 2012: Portaferry and Strangford Information Sheet. *Strangford Lough and Lecale Partnership.* Portaferry.

Tele Atlas., 2009: Google Maps [online]. Author accessed in October 2013. *Available* at <http://maps.google.co.uk>.

Simon, T., 1980: *Jupiter's Travels.* Penguin Books.

Simon, T., 2007: *Dreaming of Jupiter.* Sphere.

SMR: Sites and Monuments Record. *Environment and Heritage Service: Built Heritage.* http://www.doeni.gov.uk/niea/built-home.htm. Department of the Environment, Northern Ireland.

Stewart, L., 2012: Unearthing the mystery of what lies beneath the ancient Mound of Down. Belfast Telegraph. Belfast.

Waterman, D. M., 1967: The Early Christian Churches and Cemetery at Derry, Co. Down. *Ulster Journal of Archaeology,* Volume 30, *pp 53 – 75.* Belfast.

Waterman, D. M., 1967: A Note on Strangford Castle, County Down. *Ulster Journal of Archaeology,* Volume 30, *pp 83 – 86.* Belfast.

Waterman, D. M., 1971: Romanesque Stone-Carving from Killyleagh, Co. Down. *Ulster Journal of Archaeology Third Series.* Volume 34 *pp 110.* Belfast.

Index

132

Clachan's 'Historic Irish Journeys' series

Travels In Ireland - J.G. Kohl
This is a very readable account by a German visitor of his tour around Ireland immediately before the Great Famine.

Disturbed Ireland – 1881 - Bernard Becker
A series of letters written as the author travelled around the West of Ireland, visiting key places in the 'Land War'. We meet Captain Boycott and other members of the gentry, as well as a range of small farmers and peasants.

A Journey throughout Ireland, During the Spring, Summer and Autumn of 1834 - Henry D. Inglis
Inglis travels Ireland attempting to answer the question, 'is Ireland and improving country?' using discussion with landlords, manufacturers and tenants plus his own insightful observations.

The West Of Ireland: Its Existing Condition and Prospects - Henry Coulter
This is a collection of letters from *Saunders's News-Letter* relating to the condition and prospects of the people of the West of Ireland after the partial failure of the harvests of the early 1860s.

Highways and Byways in Donegal and Antrim - Stephen Gwynn
Take this book with you as you travel around Donegal and the Glens of Antrim and you will find that you journey not only over land, but also over time.

* * * * * * *

Clachan 'Local History' Series

Henry Coulter's account has been sub-divided for the convenience of local and family historians.
The West Of Ireland: Its Existing Condition and Prospects, Part 1, by Henry Coulter. This is an extract from the complete edition dealing with Athlone, Co. Clare and Co. Galway.

The West Of Ireland: Its Existing Condition and Prospects, Part 2, by Henry Coulter. This is an extract from the complete edition dealing with Co. Mayo.

The West Of Ireland: Its Existing Condition and Prospects, Part 3, by Henry Coulter. The final extract from the complete edition dealing with Counties Co Sligo, Donegal, Leitrim and Roscommon.

* * * * * * *

J.G.Kohl's account has been sub-divided for the convenience of local and family historians.
Travels in Ireland – Part 1, takes us through Edgeworthtown, The Shannon, Limerick, Edenvale, Kilrush and Father Mathew.

Travels in Ireland – Part 2, his journey continues through Tarbet, Tralee, Killarney, Bantry, Cork, Kilkenny and Waterford.

Travels in Ireland – Part 3, this section deals with Wexford, Enniscorthy, Avoca, Glendalough and Dublin.

Travels In Ireland - Part 4 – he goes north for the last part of his journey through Dundalk, Newry, Belfast, The Antrim Coast, Rathlin, The Giant's Causeway.

Henry D. Inglis' account has also been sub-divided for the convenience of local and family historians.
A Journey throughout Ireland, During the Spring, Summer and Autumn of 1834, Part 1 takes us from Dublin. Through Wexford, Waterford and Cork.

A Journey throughout Ireland, During the Spring, Summer and Autumn of 1834, **Part 2** is an account of Kerry, Clare, Limerick and the Shannon and concludes in Athlone.

Stephen Gwynn's account has also been sub-divided for the convenience of local and family historians.
Highways and Byways in Donegal and Antrim Part One: Donegal
Highways and Byways in Donegal and Antrim Part: Two - Derry & Co. Antrim

*   *   *   *   *   *   *

Aghaidh Achadh Mór, The Face of Aghamore – edited by Joe Byrne. This is a reproduction of a title originally published in 1991 and is of enduring interest to local historians and to those with ancestral roots in East Mayo. It covers such topics as Stone Age archaeology, family history, local hedge schools, O'Carolan's connection with the parish, the Civil War and townland surveys.

Lough Corrib, Its Shores and Islands: with Notices of Lough Mask - by William R. Wilde, first published in 1867. In the words of the author: 'A work intended to … rescue from oblivion, or preserve from desecration, some of the historic monuments of the country'.

A Statistical and Agricultural Survey of the Co. of Galway – by Hely Dutton
This is a detailed description of the agricultural conditions and practices of Galway in the early 19C, including detailed chronologies of Galway officials and its governance, senior churchmen and abbeys, monasteries and convents.

A History of Sligo: Town and Country, Vol. I, by Terrence O'Rorke
This classic and well-loved history, first published in 1889, is the work of a man born and bred in Sligo. It remains a work of fascination for anyone with connections to Sligo, and is an important reference for anyone interested in the history of Ireland.

Captain Cuellar's Adventures in Connaught and Ulster, A.D. 1588,
by Francisco de Cuellar, Hugh Allingham and Robert Crawford
This is an extraordinary first-hand account of the survival of a captain of the Spanish Armada. Ship-wrecked off the Sligo coast he faces horrors and pursuit to the death. He finds sanctuary among two Irish chieftains before making his way to the North Coast of Antrim and final deliverance.

A Step Up – by Pat Nolan
This is the story of the BIM 56-footers. The book contains details on each boat, and recollections of individuals who owned and/or fished on them.

*   *   *   *   *   *   *

Ballads and Songs

Songs of the Glens of Antrim, Moiré O'Neill
These Songs of the Glens of Antrim were written by a Glenswoman in the dialect of the Glens, and chiefly for the pleasure of other Glens-people.

Away with Words, by Michael Sands
Poems of family, home, place and music in North Antrim

Clachan
Publishing
Clachan Publishing, Ballycastle, Glens of Antrim.